One Year

of

Thankful
Thursdays

One Year

of

Thankful
Thursdays

52 Unique Perspectives
Cultivating a Heart of Gratitude
And Eyes To See God Everywhere

Susan W. Brown

Published by Best Seller Publishing®, St. Augustine, FL
Best Seller Publishing® is a registered trademark.
Printed in the United States of America.
ISBN: 978-1-959840-72-5

For more information, please write:
Best Seller Publishing®
53 Marine Street
St. Augustine, FL 32084
or call 1 (626) 765-9750
Visit us online at: www.BestSellerPublishing.org

Contents

Dedication

This book is dedicated first and foremost to The One True & Living God who has seen and saved me through more fiery trials than I can count at this point. He is not *a part* of my life...He *IS* my life and I owe everything I have and am to Him.

To my amazing best friend, also called my hubby, and my 2 truly astounding kiddos that I get to do life with this side of heaven, I am truly undeserving of your level of awesomeness, but am thankful to get to call you my family and learn and grow together each day that God gives us here on earth.

To my amazing friends that truly supported me and lifted me up and encouraged me to keep going on this journey when so much tried to shut me down, you know who you are. THANK YOU from the bottom, top, middle, and sides of this squishy beating heart. I love you and am extremely and undeservingly grateful for you.

To you, reading this book, for you to know that you are NOT ALONE and are in the right place. When the world creeps in and tries to convince you otherwise, turn the volume down on the world and turn it waaaaay up on The Word. You are valued, seen, and greatly loved my friend.

What People Are Saying

Real Tangible Hope

Susan helps you turn down the noise of this world and tune into the real tangible hope that is in Christ, and gives you the roadmap to get there.

—*Patty Aubery, President, Jack Canfield Companies*
#1 NY Times Bestselling Chicken Soup for the Christian Soul

A Blessing In My Hands!!!

As a person, myself, that has gone through a lot of struggles in life, I try to look for God and keep myself busy in my own world so I don't give up so easily when more life issues happen, but I never paid so much close attention to ALL the gifts God has put in front of us to see His love and mercy towards me, His beloved child. Susan made me realize how lucky, loved, and blessed I am by reading her book. I really enjoyed this book and the chance to connect more with my Lord. Thanks Susan.

—*S.A.*
Entrepreneur and thankful reader

Worth Every Penny!!

I have taken the time to read this book and it is pure joy. Currently, having a parent who is ill can overwhelm you mentally and physically. Susan Brown brings everything back in perspective for me. Going back to the core and creating a gracious attitude towards anything that I face. I love the scriptures after each chapter. This is very helpful as I pray and meditate. I would highly recommend this book to anyone who needs a different perspective about gratitude. Please get the book. You will not be disappointed!!

—*Kristy*
Educator, Caregiver, Child of God

A Beautiful Space and Reminder!

Life can get soooooo busy. This book is the perfect reminder to focus on gratitude and joy!!! Thank you for creating this!!!! I am looking forward to sitting down with my girls to do this together.

—*Rose Parma*
Speaker, Pastor, Educator, Christian Life & Business Coach

Beyond an Inspiring Reminder of Who We Are and What we have been given!

In a time of upheaval and challenges comes a reminder of the wonders and grace The Lord gives us. Thank you Susan for giving us a wonderful perspective on what our eyes can see and beyond. Thankful for your willingness to look into your life lessons. Such an inspiration and challenge for me to look at my own wonders around me and find just how grateful I am as I walk throughout my day.

—*Judy Best*
Mom, Wife, Child of The King

One Thousand Stars! HIGHLY Recommend!

Every once in a while you are blessed with people in your life that fall in that "privileged to know" category, and Susan Brown, is without hesitation one of those people. Yes she is multi-talented, an awesome friend, mom and teacher, resilient beyond description, sweet, beautiful, smart, and creative, but that's not why she falls into that category. She's real. And her genuineness of character and purity of soul leap off these pages straight into your heart, always always pointing you higher, right to His Face! She has eyes to see Jesus in the everyday, and she has so kindly shared with us how to do the same. That's why. One Thousand Stars. Highly Recommend!

—*Lisa M.*
Christian Counselor, Poodle Mom,
Child of The One True King

Amazing!

Susan Brown is an amazing Christ filled woman. She is inspiring, loving, and very unique. The book is wonderful and highly recommended!

—Sandy VanTubergen
Jesus Lover, Grateful Reader

The GEM Of The Year!

We live in a world where negativity is so prevalent. How refreshing is it to dig into the everyday things that we so often take for granted? Susan Brown has a unique ability to look at the mundane and find the blessing. It is her special gift! This is a refreshing reminder that in every dark cloud there is a silver lining. If you are looking for reminders on how to be thankful, this book is it! Not only that, but Susan gives all the credit and thanks to Our Creator, who deserves all the honor, glory, and praise. Read this book, and gift it to everyone who's life you want to bless. One Year Of Thankful Thursdays is a real GEM, and so is the author.

—Wendy Wallace
Christian Life Coach & Content Creator

A Quiet Place Of Joy

I really enjoyed this book of Susan's. It's a lovely part of my morning every Thursday before I go to work. Not only does it help me in my gratitude practice, it also makes me think about things on a different level.

—Cindy S.
One Year Of Thankful Thursdays Fan

Fresh Perspective

I highly recommend this to anyone looking for a fresh perspective. Susan has a way of coming alongside you and giving you just what you need to change your view point and ultimately your life, one Thankful Thursday at a time. Grab a copy. You won't regret it.

—Customer and Grateful Reader

RELATABLE!

This book totally caught my eye. It's so nice to know others are living to the fullest in gratitude. This was written out as if my own heart spilled out and Susan picked it up and put it into words! So GRATEFUL for her sharing her gifts that God has given to her and that she in return gives all glory to Him!!

—*Carlicia H.*
Gratitude Practicer, Entrepreneur

What an amazing book!

I love, love, love this! It gives you a fresh outlook on how you should view life! It can take one view of your life and change it completely by simply changing the way you think about it and what you focus on! Love the way this is written, love the title, and love the message behind it! Excellent product and I think everyone could benefit by reading it! Kudos to you for trying to change the world one mind at a time!

—*R.S., Thankful Reader*

Mind Medicine

This is a wonderful book to shift your perspective to one that is full of more gratitude. What stood out to me the most is the unique ways that the author gets you to think about how you can cultivate appreciation in your life and how she ties in spirituality into all of it.

—*Morgan Purdy*
Psychotherapist, Yoga Teacher

A Must Read!!!!

This book is a MUST READ! The author does an amazing job sharing how/why we should be Thankful in all things through God. Sharing her personal life experiences makes this book relatable to many. Great job to the author! Loved this book!!

—*Lisa Stowe, Vintage Shop Owner Extraordinaire*

Mind-Blowingly Amazing!!!

This book lets you, the reader, look at things in a whole different perspective and the real life personal stories from the author let's you know you're not alone in this world. I love the faith centered inspirations this book gave me. If you haven't read it yet, don't wait. Get it today!!

—Ginnie Knight
Author, Entrepreneur, Overcomer

Very Unique Perspective!

This is such a unique perspective on gratefulness. You already know the list of things we spout off every November. Try looking at some truly unique ideas for your growth and happiness. These chapters each walk you through maintaining a grateful heart no matter what your day brings. An amazing read.

—Texas Gal
Grateful Reader

5 Plus Stars!

There are times in your life when something comes to you and makes the biggest difference. This book was truly a blessing. I picked it up and could not put it down. I highly recommend this book and 5 stars are not enough.

—Grateful Changed Reader

Always a Positive Perspective for a Negative World

Absolutely love this book. I found it amazing that so many of her personal stories are relatable to mine. She reminds me that God is always there and to recognize and be thankful for the great things in life, but be thankful for mundane things just as much.

—Abbey Touchette
Massage Therapist, Daughter of The King

Helps Adjust the Attitude!

This is a great book to own and share with others. The author does a great job at highlighting that we should be thankful for EVERYTHING!! So easy to get lost in the "woe is me" mentality. This book will help you snap right out of it!! Very well done and I highly recommend this read!!

—*Angela R.S.*
Educator, Mom, Advocate for Truth

Gratitude is easier with this book. A Moodlifter.

This book really makes writing and believing grateful thoughts easier. Gratitude journals are effective but tough to stick with. This helps because it shares simple things and Christian writings from The Bible. Great gift and so glad I received it.

—*Carol H.*
Mom, Overcomer

Helpful Encouragement to Christian Pilgrims

Susan Brown's One Year of Thankful Thursdays is an inspired look at life by noticing the simple things in life. Through everyday ideas and objects she takes us to The Lord with thankful hearts. I have read this book through and find it unique among other books I have read. Even though life is hard at times, the author encourages us to take a deeper look at life through a spiritual lens with thanksgiving. I highly recommend this book to the serious believing Christian.

—*D. Wheeler*
Percussionist, Woodworker, Educator

Full of Wisdom!

My soul sister so well writes this book. We knew each other through the blogging community, and I always admire her honesty and wisdom. She writes from the heart, and she always makes you see things that we even take for granted. Some examples are thankful for the trashcans, the circles, the turtles, the water pipes, which is my favorite.

Reading her book is like an additional or another instrument or water-pipe God sent to me, so I get the message correctly. I will be confident of what I am doing and assure me that God is with me through my journey.

—*April Rode*
Travel Blogger, Influencer, Entrepreneur, Mom, Overcomer

Grateful & Faithful

I highly recommend this book! The author's faithfulness and positivity is a breath of fresh air. In a year of such negativity and uncertainty...we all need a gentle reminder of all the little things we have to be thankful for. I bought a book for me and a few others to give as gifts.

—*Kristen B.*
Custom Furniture Shop Owner, Entrepreneur, Mom, and Wife

Phenomenal Book FULL OF Encouragement

Gratitude is an amazing thing. There is so much negativity in the world and we are all in need of reminders that help us to be thankful and gracious. I love the way that the author uses her own experiences to encourage us. This book can be read as a daily devotional, once a week as a guide to grati-tude, or even in the small group setting to encourage one another. I love this book and cannot recommend it enough! I will be purchasing more copies for friends and family!

—*Lindsey Schnute*
Wife, Mom, Nurse, Caregiver

This book grabs your attention, engages you in each Thankful Thursday, and is a delight!

I have just received this book and couldn't wait to write a review. Susan has a way of causing you all to see we have to be thankful for. I never thought of being thankful for shadows. With what she wrote and scriptures, that will catch your eye with different fonts, you realize how we should be thankful for shadows. Susan's writing captures your attention, and caused me to underline and sometimes double star. She asks questions where I write my answer. I also like how Susan has left room on the pages, to write.

For me writing notes and all help me to sink things in. I am engaging with the author, and making sure I chew on the writing that I need to learn and do. Susan makes you think and evaluate your life. I don't want to put it down. Great book. Worth it! _Update:_ This book will help those with anxiety, depression, stress, struggles, and more. It helps put your focus in the right place, God. It helps you develop an attitude of gratitude! I can't find my original copy so I bought another one.

—*Debra Sloane*
Caregiver, Mom, OYOTT Fan

A True Blessing, Every Word!

I absolutely love this book! It will uplift your spirits and put a smile on your face! This has been such a difficult year in my career field. I am reminded of all the many things to be grateful for. Susan and her family are dear friends and have been for 20+ years. To know her is to love her.

—*Michele Leonard*
Wife, Mom, Child of God

Best Book for the year

Such an uplifting, inspiring book. Very well written. I start my day reading this book every morning.

—*Julie Wamble*
Hairdresser, Wife, & Mom

You Need This Book!

We all need to be reminded, especially now, to be thankful for everything. This book was sent to me at at time when I really needed reminding that everything in life is a gift. Do yourself a favor and buy this book. As you read each day, take the time to absorb it. My favorite had to do with the sea turtles!

—*Angela Mcmann Ruth*
Wife, Mom, Overcomer

See The Miracles

We are all so busy with our busy-ness that we miss so much. This book goes through each day noticing something different that is just part of our lives, but when we take time to see, it is a thing of beauty and significance in filling our lives with joy. Thank you for your thoughts on the miracles all around us.

—*M. Travis*
Grateful Reader

Blessed from the moment I opened the first page

The inscription on the first page was Numbers 6:24-26. My daughter in love and I had just exchanged birthday gifts. She gifted me with One Year of Thankful Thursdays, and the card I gave her had the exact same verse. I knew this was His gift to me, to her, too. In Susan's introduction I felt as if we were immediately connected. Her humor, her honesty, and her verse choices drew me in on Thankful Thursday #1. I can't wait to share this timely book with all my girls, near and far.

—*Veronica Lynn Berry*
Grateful Reader, OYOTT Fan

Exceptional writing will warm your heart!

Gratitude, the quality that expresses appreciation, prompts the return of kindness, and gets us thinking about something other than ourselves. No surprise that Susan Brown exquisitely captured this profound quality with such grace and practicality as her life is the epitome of giving and being thankful. Susan's exceptional writing makes you feel like you're chatting with your childhood best friend while getting expert advice. You will delight in One Year of Thankful Thursdays and be sure to keep it close....as it will warm your heart, make you laugh and teach you life long beautiful lessons all in one sitting.

—*Tracie Marciniak*
Entrepreneur, Author, Speaker, Business Strategist Extraordinaire

Powerful Insights!

I am thankful for Susan Brown and the gift of beautiful insights she has shared with us. I loved this particular one that was fresh for me, "Even in the valley we are MOVING...we are walking THROUGH IT!" Susan has given me new eyes to see.

—*Grateful Changed Reader*

An Amazing Perspective!

How could anyone forget Susan or the gathering of women that day. It was a morning like no other. Susan brought an amazing perspective to so many of God's everyday creations... a new way of looking at so many blessings surrounding us every day . The mundane things of life that really aren't mundane. On Thursdays, I text my special friend because Susan's book reminds me of my friendship with her and the amazing morning we all shared. Thank you, Susan, for being you and for sharing your thoughts with all of us.

—*Camille Luscher*
Daughter of The King, World Traveler

Foreword

All I can say is that Susan's book, "One Year of Thankful Thursdays" has impacted my life more than any book (outside the Bible) ever has! Let me clarify further. I have had a love affair with books of all types all my life. I have always loved books and am never without a current book that I have my nose in. As a child I would escape to my backyard and climb to the top of the Magnolia tree with my horsebook, usually one of Marguerite Henry's Classic horse books illustrated by the incredible watercolors of Wesley Dennis to read in peace and quiet.

I have loved so many books. But "One Year of Thankful Thursdays" has gotten into my heart and soul. I have shared so many of these books with friends because one "Thursday" had spoken to me enough to share with a particular friend who I knew would get so much comfort and encouragement from reading Susan's words and the attached scriptures.

I have lost track of the number of books I have gifted. I've shared with family, friends, folks who didn't particularly like me, and a few complete strangers. When I feel God prodding my shoulder I have learned to not question, be obedient to his prod and trust the results to Him. No one has thrown the book back at me, and new relationships are being created and existing relationships strengthened. I have given this book to several friends who had become estranged from me and in the giving, relationships are being restored.

Thank you Susan for obeying God and getting vulnerable enough to write this life-changing book. Thank you God.

—*Foncie Bullard*
People Magnet, Avid Reader, Horse Lover

Introduction

In this day and age there seems to be an extra measure of complaining, condescending, belittling and more than we want to mention here with regards to negativity.

It seems that somehow we have gotten so caught up in the "Gotta Hustle" mindset and chasing the "bigness" of fame and fortune that we have missed the absolute magnitude of the beauty that is right in front of us.

How often do you stop and marvel at something as simple as a rooftop, a tree trunk, a pipe, and so many more truly amazing gifts that we have been given?

Have you thought about how we are to celebrate our differences and lift one another up towards greatness instead of trying to win and outshine one another? A thankful and humble heart is the first step towards that measure.

There is a wave of change coming. If you stop for a moment, listen with the pulse of your soul, you can almost feel it...it's a palpable stampede of beauty, positivity, lifting up, encouragement, and inspiration that's on the horizon!

Yes, it's coming, but it has to start with you and me!

One day I won't be here, and you won't either, but even that doesn't have to be a negative thing. That should lead us not into a rabbit hole of worry or angst, but instead an unbelievable rabbit hole of gratitude and wonder for this very moment!

I have learned so much from different stages in my life, whether as a child, single adult, married with no kids, and married with children. One thing I have learned over the course of my life is that people are people wherever you live, whatever age they are, and whatever station in life they are in.

They all matter. They should all be celebrated, listened to, seen, appreciated and accepted.

Gratitude truly changes EVERYTHING. It gives us eyes to actually SEE, and a heart that can LOVE regardless of what is around us.

It comes from a place of acknowledging that you don't understand and know everything, but that you don't have to in order to be grateful for it. Humility and grace are key ingredients to this recipe.

I will be honest with you...some of the things I am thankful for I actually don't like, but we are told to give thanks in all things. I find great comfort and peace in just offering up thanksgiving for it all, knowing it is all a part of His plan and therefore I can trust the providence that it leads to.

Being thankful for what the world would call the small things brings you back to a childlike wonder and to be honest with you, can even give you great joy and make you a little giddy. So be forewarned, you may experience great joy while embarking on this journey.

There are also some difficult ones, so there may be tears.

They are all a part of our journey. This life is not a destination. There is not a final place we get to where we can say, "oh yup..I have this all figured out."

In fact, what if we decided to use the word LIFE as an acronym?

Live
Intentionally
Fully
Everyday

If we go about life with intention, it is so much easier to see the gratitude we should have for each and every blessing that we have been missing along the way.

I love to be intentional about looking at the everyday things, finding beauty everywhere, and thanking God for it all.

The way the curtains in my bedroom wave from the top to the bottom in just one little section due to the air blowing through the vent. Yes, I am thankful for air and that visual reminder of it cooling our home and giving us respite from the heat.

When the freezer stopped working recently and there was ruined food in the freezer and water all over the floor, I became so thankful for a working freezer most of the time and that we still had enough food. It was a visual reminder of how He provides so generously for us everyday.

Thanksgiving as an everyday routine is all about changing your PERSPECTIVE.

It's focusing on what you DO have and the heightened awareness of the blessings, both seen, and unseen that surround you every moment of every day.

This book was born for a few reasons.

One was that some readers of my original blog and social media kept requesting I put one of my social media themed days, Thankful Thursday, in book format.

Another of the reasons is that for me, on a deeply personal level, being thankful has completely changed my life. It has helped me view things from a different vantage point and overcome the darkness of depression and anxiety that threatens to pull me down. It is a fight against the darkness.

Being thankful no matter what is a way of standing up and choosing hope and choosing to live fully and seek God regardless of what surrounds me!

It was also born out of the fact that I get kind of tired of the whole "Thankful Thursdays" in November that everyone shares on social media. Here in our country, due to Thanksgiving being on a Thursday in November, it has become a popular practice to share a Thankful Thursday post on social media ONLY IN NOVEMBER. It's usually the typical stuff: faith, family, food, and friends.

And while there is nothing wrong with that, and there are very good intentions and heart behind it, *it left me wondering...is that the end of our scope... our vision?*

Do we not SEE so much more?

The deeper stuff, the seemingly mundane and ordinary stuff, and how it all points to Him?

Is our scope of giving thanks limited to only one month of the entire year? We then limit that to one day of the week? We have way more than 4 things to be thankful for without a doubt!

Let's kick that notion of only having Thankful Thursdays in November to the curb and have Thankful Thursday every Thursday of the year! Who knows? If you like this book, maybe I will do a Thankful Every Day Of The Year book next?!

It's all about taking those perspective glasses out, dusting them off, and maybe seeing clearly for the first time what is right in front of you and that it all points to Him, our Lord and Savior. You start to see that everything really can be viewed through a heavenly perspective. Nothing is out of the realm of possibility, no matter how unusual, for pointing to the One who made us to seek Him out in all the details of life!

Be grateful and watch your entire mindset, perspective, and life change! There is always, always, always something to be thankful for!

Welcome to the journey!

Thankful Thursday #1

Today I am thankful for SHADOWS!

As a child I loved watching finger shadows on the wall,
and found it fascinating.

As I grew older, shadows became something that seemed more
of a dark thing and a place I didn't want to be.

What I have learned is something so crazy outrageous
that it brightens the entire idea of shadows!

All a shadow is, is a dark area produced because of an
object coming between rays of light and a surface.

Shadows are such a powerful reminder that there is light behind the object.

The darkness of the object blocking the light from that very spot only enables the light to do its job even more so by casting the light all around the object so that it, in fact, illuminates the shape creating a shadow.

So, that is all we need right?

Sometimes if you feel like you are lost in the shadows, do not lose
heart! In fact, you have a very intense Light that is shining all
around you and behind you. It's shining all over the surface and
has got you fully illuminated whether or not you see it.

Shadows are such a powerful finger pointing towards the light.

The darkness of the shadow reminds us of the light and
it becomes all the more beautiful because of it!

Light is incredible and is capable of some pretty powerful and incredible things! The next time you see a shadow think of how the light is what makes it all possible!

Stand in the light and be thankful for the shadows!

SCRIPTURES FOR THE DAY

PSALM 63:7 is super cool to imagine,
**"For You have been my help, and
IN THE SHADOW OF YOUR WINGS
I will sing for joy."**

Wow...just wow...imagine that...standing under His wings of
protection and singing for joy because you are in His shadow!

PSALM 36:7 reminds us that He has us protected in the shadows,
**"How precious is Your steadfast love, O God!
The children of mankind TAKE REFUGE
IN THE SHADOW OF YOUR WINGS."**

*ISAIAH 9:2 reminds us if we are feeling lost
in the shadows, just wait for it...*
**"The people who walked in darkness have seen a great light;
those who dwelt in a land of deep darkness,
ON THEM HAS LIGHT SHINED."**

**YES, I am thankful for shadows because they remind
us that there is light behind us and all around us!**

Thankful Thursday #2

Today I'm so thankful for MY PERSON.

I'm thankful for the struggles and hard times we have been through because they made us dig deeper, reach up, change and grow. There have been so many through the years and many dark deep trials that only he watched me walk through and stood by my side and held my hand.

I'm thankful most of all that he obviously is a maniac for being married to me for over 22 years and hasn't run for the hills yet! He continues to support me and be my biggest fan.

Who are you thankful for today?

Your friend? A co-worker? A kind soul in the local coffee shop? Tell that person today you are thankful for them.

We aren't guaranteed tomorrow so tell that person what they mean to you. And, I am super thankful for *you* coming along on this journey with me and that you are a part of my life.

Are you misbelieving you are alone in not having "a person" because you are single or without a family for any number of various reasons?

Oh my friend, that is NOT THE CASE!

You have a best friend, "a person", a redeemer, and lover of your soul in the Highest King of The Universe.

He will be "your person". He is as real as anyone else.

Although I will be the first to admit it isn't fun that we can't touch Him in person and run into His arms and sob wildly like we need to sometimes.

But let Him in...He is right there and always has been.

SCRIPTURES FOR THE DAY

JAMES 4:8a reminds us,
"Draw near to God, and
HE WILL DRAW NEAR TO YOU."

I JOHN 3:1a tells us,
"See what kind of love the Father has given to us, that
WE SHOULD BE CALLED CHILDREN OF GOD;
and so we are."

HEBREWS 4:15 paints a beautiful picture for us,
"For WE DO NOT HAVE A HIGH PRIEST WHO IS UNABLE
TO SYMPATHIZE WITH OUR WEAKNESSES,
but one who in every respect has been tempted
as we are, yet was without sin."

Be so encouraged today that you do "have a person"
whether or not you knew it before this moment.

He loves you in a way that would quite literally
blow your mind and change your entire perspective
if you could even fathom 1/10 of it!

Thankful Thursday #3

Today I am so thankful for the
"NOT PICTURE PERFECT AND MESSY" moments.

It's too easy to get caught up in what the world mandates...pretty light-filled pictures and perfectly manicured moments.

So, I'm sharing just a regular picture on a cloudy day where we made beautiful messy memories!

This was from Mother's Day when we were at the beach and the girls were busy digging a hole and tunnel hopefully (their precious words, not mine.).

It was beautiful, messy, not-picture-perfect, and the kind of moments I wish I could capture in a bottle and hang onto forever!

Be thankful for the REAL, not photo edited (no filter here), sometimes messy journey that is YOUR life.

After all, when we look back, it's the messy moments that are usually the most precious and easier to grasp in our minds. Then we realize that those are the moments that make up this beautiful IRREPLACEABLE once in a lifetime gift called LIFE!

SCRIPTURES FOR THE DAY

It's all a part of the journey and COLOSSIANS 3:14 reminds us,
"And above all these put on love, which binds everything together IN PERFECT HARMONY."

ECCLESIASTES 3:12 reminds us to just enjoy the moments so that we aren't so caught up in the "just right" version of life,
"I perceived that there is nothing better for them than to BE JOYFUL and to do good as long as they live;"

Be thankful for these messy moments! It all comes together in the end in perfect harmony!

Thankful Thursday #4

Today I am so thankful for SEASHELLS...especially the broken, chipped, or damaged ones.

I love these type of seashells more because they are such a visual reminder of how God takes our brokenness and sees each one of us.

None of our brokenness is wasted…not one iota of it is lost anywhere. I am thankful that He sees this broken seashell and loves me still!

It's the broken or chipped shells that grab my attention against all the other perfect ones that may blend in and look the same. There's something about the imperfection that draws me in and makes me want to know more about this shell and where the waves have tossed it, how many feet it has avoided, if anyone has tossed it to the ground unwanted.

It's really no different than people in that sense is it? None of us are perfect anyway. Some try to pretend more than others. The ones that have the pain, trials, and have been in the trenches seem to have a bit more character, perseverance, abiding faith and therefore beauty. There's something about those people that draws me in. I want to know them, learn more, and listen well. That's where the beauty lies after all.

SCRIPTURES FOR THE DAY

*Maybe we are drawn to those chipped and seemingly broken ones
because PSALM 34:18 reminds us of something truly beautiful,*
"The Lord is NEAR TO THE BROKENHEARTED
and saves the crushed in spirit."

*2 CORINTHIANS 12:9 is an acknowledgment of the chips
and the beauty and power that comes from it.*
"But he said to me, "My grace is sufficient for you, for
MY POWER IS MADE PERFECT IN WEAKNESS."
Therefore I will boast all the more gladly about my
weaknesses, so that the power of Christ
may rest upon me."

Yes, I am thankful for those beautiful chipped,
damaged, and imperfect seashells. They provide such
beautiful life lessons when we put on our perspective
glasses and view them through a heavenly lens.

Thankful Thursday #5

While it may sound bizarre, today I am
thankful for TREE TRUNKS.

Most of their lives they are responsible for holding the weight of the branches and taking whatever nutrients they can get from the ground to help serve that purpose.

But if one day, that tree should fall or get knocked down, it doesn't just vanish, it just changes its purpose a bit.

The new purpose may include being a home to the many critters that need a safe habitat, while also offering a weary traveler a place to rest.

I am struck with how similar this is with our own lives.

For a time we were young and needed support. Then as we grow stronger and more able, we stand on our own and eventually support others.

What happens if life takes a crazy turn and knocks us down? We find another way to serve…that's what we do.

God didn't design our lives to look like one stage our entire life. Think of the knocked down stage as a place to seek others to offer comfort to as they need a safe place.

Thankful for tree trunks and the life lessons they offer us.

Thankful for the God who made the trees and made us to seek Him out in every detail of life.

SCRIPTURES FOR THE DAY

PSALM 96:12 tells us,
"Let the fields be jubilant, and everything in them;
LET ALL THE TREES OF THE FOREST SING FOR JOY."

When life has taken a turn and you aren't sure what to do next,
PSALM 32:8 reminds us,
"I WILL INSTRUCT YOU and teach you
IN THE WAY YOU SHOULD GO;
I will counsel you with my loving eye on you."

**I am so thankful you are here, alive, and present. Go seek
out the beauty where you are today in the normally unseen
places, and know that you are always seen by the God
of the universe who loves you with an unfailing love.**

Thankful Thursday #6

Today I am thankful for the
"FADE AND BLUR LENS"
that God uses when He looks at me.

Much like this picture where the focus is on the very blossom right in front
of you and not the rest that it's connected to is how God sees you and me.

It's so hard to wrap my mind around that so often when I am tempted to think that I am just a big compilation of my history and past.

That's NOT how God sees us friend!

He looks at us through the lens of His perfect Son who
He willingly gave up FOR YOU AND ME!

I have made so many mistakes: some small, some big, and some hurtful. I tend to self-loathe and want to crawl out of my own skin at times, BUT GOD.

His vantage point and lens brings me back reminding me He sees me through Jesus and has the strongest fade and blur effect we could hope for!

Today, put away the self-doubt, negativity, frustrations, and pain and be reminded that God doesn't connect you to your past or mistakes when He looks at you.

Our history is part of His Story and that is right and true, and we have it to remind us how far we have come and to mold and shape us.

Be so encouraged today friend that God puts on the Jesus level fade lens when He looks at you!

He doesn't see a nasty disgusting mess that is unsaveable or beyond repair.

He sees a highly treasured, one-of-a-kind, beautiful human being that He loves and gave up everything for!

SCRIPTURES to prove this lens is accurate!

PSALM 36:1 tells us what happens with our mistakes,
"Blessed is the one
whose transgressions are forgiven,
WHOSE SINS ARE COVERED."

ISAIAH 43:25 is a beautiful picture of the fade and blur lens,
"I, even I, am He who
BLOTS OUT YOUR TRANSGRESSIONS,
for my own sake, and
REMEMBERS YOUR SINS NO MORE."

ROMANS 8:1 reminds us of this promise,
"There is therefore now NO CONDEMNATION
for those who are in Christ Jesus."

Go have a beautiful day knowing that today, right now, God sees *you* with the Jesus level "fade and blur lens" and *you* are a beautiful creation highly valued!

Thankful Thursday #7

I could jump out of my skin for what I am thankful for today!

It's AIR! Today I am crazy thankful for AIR!

So very thankful for something I cannot see, but can see what it does. I cannot touch it, but can feel it when it moves.

I need it every minute of every hour of every day and
without it I would die.

Oh my AIR! How wonderful and beautiful and special and unappreciated
it is until we are so desperate for it, it's the only thing we can think about.

When we first moved to Texas, I had major breathing problems every fall. They were so severe, I would land in urgent care getting emergency breathing treatments. I became the owner of an inhaler and an Epi Pen. In those moments of desperation, I guarantee you I was solely focused on breathing and how I would give up everything I had, except my faith and family, just for the next breath.

Isn't AIR so much like THE HOLY SPIRIT?!

We can't see Him, but can see the effects when He moves.

We can't touch Him but we can surely feel Him and His presence.

And we surely need Him every moment of every hour of every day!

We are definitely hyper-aware of our need for
Him when desperation kicks in and we are needing
emergency treatments and help from Him!

In my humble mind, it's no mistake that God designed our bodies to be so dependent on air.

I mean think about it for a minute. He could have made us dependent on water, but He didn't. We can see and touch and somewhat hang onto water.

Maybe, *just maybe,* He made our physical bodies dependent on something we cannot see or touch so our spiritual minds and hearts will learn to do the same as we lean on the Holy Spirit for guidance and sustaining us.

SCRIPTURES FOR THE DAY

JOB 33:4 puts it so beautifully,
"The SPIRIT of God has MADE ME, and the BREATH OF THE ALMIGHTY gives me life."

JOHN 3:8 is a beautiful description of air and The Spirit,
"THE WIND BLOWS WHERE IT WISHES, and you hear its sound, but you do not know where it comes from or where it goes. So it is with everyone who is BORN OF THE SPIRIT."

2 CORINTHIANS 5:5 tells us He gave us The Holy Spirit as a GIFT,
"He who has prepared us for this very thing is God, who has GIVEN US THE SPIRIT AS A GUARANTEE."

However you are breathing right now, I am so very thankful that you are!

Take a deep breath in and be reminded of the beauty of the very things we cannot see and thank God for sustaining you!

Thankful Thursday #8

Today I am thankful for the gift of SLEEP!

I think in our non-stop culture sleep can be something that is looked down upon because of the idea that "you aren't being productive if you are sleeping" or the always hustle mindset of "you have to work, work, work so you can get ahead".

I have been guilty, in the past, of not looking forward to sleep for another reason entirely. I just love life and enjoy being busy (most of the time) and there's so much life to live and so much to do and experience I just want to be up doing it!

BUT...

There's a real danger in not getting enough sleep or making sleep a priority.

Just as God designed the seasons of the year to flow in a natural rhythm and even the 24 hour period in a day to have a cycle, so our bodies were designed with a natural rhythm as well.

Take a step back, recharge by getting some extra sleep, and see the world and life fresh and anew.

Our bodies need the sleep in order for our minds and bodies to function at peak capacity.

I have been overly exhausted recently. I knew it was affecting every area of my life as I was short with people, my body was extra torn down from my usual workouts, and I was falling asleep at random times in mid conversation.

So, for the next 2 mornings, I planned to sleep in. Instead of waking at 4, I slept in until 6:30 and it made a massive difference in those 2 days and after.

It can change not only your perspective, but also massively increase your productivity, energy, and attitude.

Sleep truly is a gift and we should treat it as such and use it wisely.

SCRIPTURES FOR THE DAY

PSALM 127:2 reminds us that
"HE GRANTS SLEEP
to those He loves."

This does not at all imply that if you aren't sleeping He doesn't love you.

What it does imply is this. It's OK and good to throw that worry
off...lie down...sleep...it's good and healthy for you!

PSALM 4:8 reminds us how we are to go to sleep...in peace,
"IN PEACE, I will LIE DOWN AND SLEEP, for you
alone, O Lord, make me dwell in safety."

Have a beautiful Thursday as you are
thanking God for the gift of sleep.

Please know this today...you are worth fighting
for says the King of the Universe who never sleeps.
(Psalm 121:4)

Thankful Thursday #9

Today I am so thankful for PIGGYBACK RIDES.

I'm thankful for the heavenly picture they paint for us.

I love watching my oldest lovingly offer my youngest a piggyback ride when she gets too tuckered out. It gives her a little reprieve and makes her feel loved and protected.

I also love watching my man give piggyback rides to his girls to give them a rest and boost right when they need it. It also offers them that reminder that they don't have to do it all. It lovingly reassures them that they aren't alone and that he will willingly carry and protect them. It puts him in front taking the brunt of what lies ahead while she is safely and knowingly trusting wherever He goes.

Isn't this such a picture of our Heavenly Daddy?

Again, don't take my word for it, His word confirms all of this in these beautiful reminders.

SCRIPTURES FOR THE DAY

DEUTERONOMY 31:8 beautifully depicts God being out in front,
"THE LORD is the one WHO GOES AHEAD OF YOU.
HE WILL BE WITH YOU.
He will not fail or forsake you.
Do not fear or be dismayed."

Do you see how my man has got her hemmed in front and back
by his arms being behind him holding onto her tightly?
Well how about PSALM 139:5 tells us,
"YOU HEM ME IN BEHIND AND BEFORE,
you have laid your hand upon me."

JOSHUA 1:9 reminds us we are never alone!
"Have I not commanded you? Be strong and courageous.
Do not be afraid. Do not be discouraged, for the Lord your
God WILL BE WITH YOU WHEREVER YOU GO."

Can't you just PICTURE that?

PSALM 68:19 reminds us He is carrying us AND our struggles,
"Praise be to the Lord, to God our Savior, who
daily BEARS OUR BURDENS."

Do you see it now? Do you see how piggybacks are such a
heavenly picture of our loving Heavenly Daddy carrying
us and leading us through this journey called life?

Yes, I am thankful for piggyback rides and how they
point to The One who made us and loves us always.

Thankful Thursday #10

I am humbly thankful for FREEDOM!

I am beyond blessed to get to live where we know that FREEDOM is and was IN NO WAY free. It was and continues to be bought and paid for with the blood of brave men and women who boldly stand to protect what they love.

We love our country BUT, there is another FREEDOM so much bigger than this or any country's FREEDOM.

None of us are more special than any other human just because we happen to be born where we were born.

There are people of every land (including ours) that suffer and experience the feeling of not being free whether that's in an abusive relationship, having no money to buy food or pay the bills, and so many other ways, or even actually being imprisoned.

So, today I am obviously thankful for the beautiful blessings of living in the land of the FREE. I tell every soldier every chance I get, "Thank You for Your Service!" as should we all!

But even that points to something even bigger...

> *It paints a beautiful picture that points to an even greater FREEDOM we are all given and it also WAS NOT FREE!*

> *It was bought and paid for with the precious blood of Christ!*

> *It's FREEDOM IN CHRIST my beautiful friend!*

> *It has been paid for ONE time with ONE perfect Savior!*

It's a ONCE and DONE extraordinary miraculous unfathomable FREEDOM that nothing else can compare to!

It's a deep abiding gift of acceptance, peace, contentment, and even joy that is YOURS for the taking.

The chains and shackles are GONE!

SCRIPTURES FOR THE DAY

GALATIANS 5:1 tells us we have been set FREE,
"It is FREEDOM that CHRIST HAS SET US FREE.
Stand firm, then, and do not let yourselves be
burdened again by a yoke of slavery."

GALATIANS 5:13 tell us what to do with this freedom,
"You my brothers and sisters were CALLED TO BE FREE.
But do not use your freedom to indulge the flesh; rather,
SERVE ONE ANOTHER HUMBLY IN LOVE."

*2 CORINTHIANS 3:17 reminds us our freedom is not
confined to circumstances or physical location,*
"Now The Lord is the Spirit, and WHERE THE SPIRIT
OF THE LORD IS, THERE IS FREEDOM."

ROMANS 8:2 reminds us we have been redeemed!
"For the law of the Spirit of Life has
SET YOU FREE IN CHRIST JESUS
from the law of sin and death."

No matter what country you live in,
whatever your circumstances may presently be,
YOU HAVE BEEN SET FREE and you get to hold
fast to that in the private depths of your soul where
no one can take that away from you EVER!

Live FREE because you truly are in the beautiful,
unseen, invisible realm where it matters most!

Thankful Thursday #11

Today I am thankful for the beautiful gift of IMAGINATION!

It gets me a little giddy like a kid thinking about imagination, especially when combined with creativity and ingenuity!

I just love that my girls see a great big ocean to cross, in their minds, and need the paddles and a life raft to cross when my stuffy adult mind only saw a pool!

Do we forget how absolutely incredible God's imagination must be?

First off, THE WORLD! I mean really?

He imagined all this and then created it from nothing!

If you want more proof that God has a wild imagination...look up some of these creatures...the Anglerfish, Yeti Crab, the Superb Bird of Paradise, and the Zebra Duiker just to name a few.

God made them all!
All of that was a part of His imagination!!
And then He formed it into being! GENESIS 2:19-20

Imagination is a beautiful blessing...when the heart and the mind come together to wonder at the works of His hand and how incredible and vast His love and creativity is!

Maybe that's why unless we become like little ones
we can't enter the kingdom of heaven.

Kids have so much of life figured out better than we do, and we need to imagine more the way they do...it can lead to creativity, growth and even joy!

SCRIPTURES FOR THE DAY

**Want actual scripture to back up proof of
His imagination?**
Ok fair enough...go read REVELATION 9!

MATTHEW 18:3
**"Truly I tell you, He said,
UNLESS YOU CHANGE AND BECOME
LIKE LITTLE CHILDREN,
you will never enter the kingdom of heaven."**

*Take a minute today to just stop, look around, ponder and
wonder at the vastness and imagination of God!*

JUST IMAGINE!

*Does it make your heart a little lighter, softer, and giddy
like it does mine? Stop the stuffiness for a minute and just imagine!*

**Go have a beautiful day my friends!
Know that you are loved and were thought of and
imagined before He even created the universe!**

Thankful Thursday #12

Today I am so very thankful for the wondrous
gift of PERSPECTIVE and the paradigm
shift it can provide if we let it!

I'm also thankful for the people God puts in our paths to allow certain moments of clarity and perspective! So, shoutout to Mike in the seat next to me on this plane ride for graciously allowing me to repeatedly lean over to take pictures and get this shot of Lake Michigan!

Perspective. It is formed by our younger years but if we take out those perspective glasses I love to refer to it can completely change in so many beautiful ways!

I am in total awe when I fly...maybe because I don't do it much, I don't know. But I do think there is an awe-inspiring childlike wonder that can be a great perspective if you think about flying in how it relates to life.

It gives us a miniscule peek into what God's view must be like. It reminds us of something bigger than ourselves and that every single person matters and that somehow we are all connected.

Being up in the air in the clouds is awe-inspiring enough!

But then, lift up the window shade, look out, and just gasp at the absolute vastness and beauty of God's creation.

The best part, for me anyway, is knowing that as He looks down on what seems to us to be a great big world, He sees me and you.

I don't mean sees like noticing you are there like we notice people in the grocery store, but SEEING YOU in the most intimate way imaginable.

It's almost unnerving until you realize how beautiful it is. He sees past the clouds, the Great Lakes, the streets, the houses, and even past your skin right to your very one-of-a-kind, none other like you in the history of the world, beautiful soul.

*He sees your thoughts, knows your insecurities and
fears, and is your biggest cheerleader still!*

*I don't know about you, but for me that humbles me in ways I
can't express to know He could even notice me amongst all the
people, look at this hot mess, SEE all of me and love me still!*

Want some scripture proof of how intensely intimate God's PERSPECTIVE
IS TOWARDS YOU?

SCRIPTURES FOR THE DAY

Go read ALL of PSALM 139!

2 Corinthians 4:18 tells us of the perspective that we should have,
**"As we LOOK NOT TO THE THINGS THAT ARE SEEN but to the
things that are unseen. For the things that are seen are transient,
but THE THINGS THAT ARE UNSEEN ARE ETERNAL."**

I SAMUEL 16:7b reminds us how God sees through it all,
**"For the Lord sees not as man sees: man looks
on the outward appearance, but
THE LORD LOOKS ON THE HEART."**

**Yes, today I am thankful for perspective and
the wonder it provides! It can open up the
eyes of our soul to REALLY SEE.**

Have a beautiful day knowing YOU ARE ONE OF A KIND!

Thankful Thursday #13

Today I am so very thankful for the
CONTRAST OF LIGHT AND DARKNESS!

How in the world would we know what light is unless there was darkness for it to penetrate?

I got this incredible picture of the moon on an evening recently and was awestruck with how much darkness surrounded it and yet still that didn't affect its light at all.

It still shines regardless of what is around it or even if it's covered temporarily by the dark clouds.

Then I looked even closer and noticed that the light wasn't just contained to the circular shape of the moon, but it's effects were being rippled through the darkness.

That is so exactly like scripture and life, isn't it friend?

We aren't called to focus on the darkness and thereby allow our light to be affected by the darkness.

Not at all!

We are called to be the light and let that light permeate the darkness we encounter, and make sure not to turn it down or flicker, but to shine brightly whether surrounded by light or darkness.

Be comforted and encouraged my friend...just as the moon lights the way for you and I at night, God does for us through this world. Psalm 18:28

He has not forgotten you or turned His back on you. He is The Light that is permeating even through the darkness.

We are called to do the same.

SCRIPTURES FOR THE DAY

JOHN 1:5 reminds us we will not be overcome,
**"THE LIGHT SHINES IN THE DARKNESS,
and the darkness has not overcome it."**

JOHN 8:12 tells us who to follow to find light,
**"When Jesus spoke again to the people, He said,
"I am the Light of the world. WHOEVER FOLLOWS
ME WILL NEVER WALK IN DARKNESS,
but will have the light of life."**

JOHN 12:46 encourages us yet again,
**"I have COME INTO THE WORLD AS LIGHT,
so that no one who believes in me should stay in darkness."**

Keep your beautiful light shining, and don't be discouraged by
this world, but be encouraged that Light wins in the end!

**So thankful for the beautiful gift of light
contrasting darkness. Go have a beautiful day
shining your light and know that you have the
King of the Universe leading the way for you!**

Thankful Thursday #14

Today I am thankful for the SETBACKS IN LIFE!

Why?

Because maybe, just maybe, they are the gateway to something
truly incredible on your amazing journey!

Recently my trainer asked me what I wanted to work on. I said I have always wanted to be able to do a handstand! Normally I scream out, "pull up training", but knowing I had to take a temporary pause while my shoulder recovers I wanted to tackle another goal of mine!

Yes I realize I am crooked, off center and my elbows should be more fully locked out, but that's not really even the point here.

Here is what you don't see in this picture. My incredible trainer teaching me from absolute zero and complete fear to a full handstand on the wall in 30 minutes!

We first practiced being upside down by doing a high pike type of position on a box with hands and head on ground.

He cautioned me that it can be disorienting and man was it! The blood rushing to your head, looking straight down in one spot (ideally between the palms of your hands) and focusing on keeping your elbows fully locked.

Then I practiced hanging upside down in a band to hold me so I can get more used to that feeling.

Each time he asked me how I was feeling I replied "scared but it's OK".

I have struggled with balance and coordination most of my life and have gotten so much better since I started working out in this gym.

I don't know how many attempts it took me to get on the wall and when I finally nailed it, a wild thought clicked in my brain!

What if this...these unattainable things...or so we thought...really are up for the taking?

You just have to view the setback as a door to a brand new beginning of something beautiful in your life!

No, I am not a fitness model or pretending to be. This is not a perfect handstand, and that's the best part. I am a regular everyday mom that has big dreams and want to encourage you to chase yours!

If I hadn't had the setback of pull up training I may never have had the courage to try this desire in my heart to do a handstand.

What setback could you be thankful for today that has opened a beautiful new beginning for you?

You can do the hard stuff that you think you can't...
just try and if you fall, you fall TRYING!

SCRIPTURES FOR THE DAY

ISAIAH 40:29 tells us what He can do with setbacks!
"HE GIVES STRENGTH TO THE WEARY
and increases the power of the weak."

ISAIAH 41:10 offers comfort when afraid!
"FEAR NOT, for I AM WITH YOU; be not dismayed, for I am
your God; I WILL STRENGTHEN YOU, I WILL HELP YOU,
I will uphold you with my righteous right hand."

2 TIMOTHY 1:7 reminds us we are to be bold in the setbacks,
"For GOD GAVE US A SPIRIT NOT OF FEAR BUT OF POWER
and love and self-control."

Yes, Today I am thankful for the setbacks in life
that teach us to dig deeper and are pointing the
way to a greater lesson in overcoming!

Thankful Thursday #15

Today I am thankful for the methodical
CHANGING OF THE CLOUDS and the lesson that provides.

I love to watch clouds change. I love seeing the different shapes in them and how they so unapologetically change to something new. Usually there is a temporary unrecognizable state as it's shifting into its new form.

This points so much to our lives if we look at it through the lens of growth.

Change is inevitable, we all know that. I think what is unusual is that our entire culture seems bent on staying with what we know…meaning…don't change…you keep doing what you have always done and just stay with that.

But life isn't like that my friend.

I have done and been so many different things in my life it's like I am a real life version of what clouds do on the daily.

I am not alone in this. How do I know this?

Because I LOVE, LOVE, LOVE to talk to people. So many of us have been through so many different things and keep growing, changing, and shifting hopefully towards something much greater and more profound as we do change.

The shifting clouds are so beautiful because that temporary unrecognizable period is what we can all identify with at some point in our lives.

When you feel the growth coming and you have learned something new and you know life is about to change.

You know those times when you feel the change coming, you sense God pressing something on your heart, or a change has happened and you are adjusting to it. It's that finding of the "new normal" that is like that unrecognizable state of the clouds shifting.

It can be hard when your friends and family question you and want to put you "in a box" and not understand the change that is happening. It's OK if you don't understand it either.

We aren't all Damascus road experiences and the more I talk to people, the more I realize those are in fact the very rare cases. None are more special than the other either. There isn't some special room in heaven for the Damascus road experiences believers.

Life is always evolving and changing just like the clouds.

Don't mourn for what it used to look like or be, but instead embrace the present shape and be thankful for what it is and be ready for more shifting ahead.

Beloved, we aren't supposed to look like one thing our whole life.

There is a great big world that God made. There are billions and billions of people He made. There are countless things to learn, ways to grow, and ways to love.

SCRIPTURES FOR THE DAY

2 CORINTHIANS 5:17 beautifully describes that
we will change into something new,
"Therefore, if anyone is in Christ, he is a new creation.
The old has passed away; behold, THE NEW HAS COME."

EZEKIAL 36:26 tells us we will actually BE different
from a spiritual heart transplant,
"And I will give you a new heart, and
A NEW SPIRIT I WILL PUT WITHIN YOU.
And I will remove the heart of stone from your
flesh and give you a heart of flesh."

ROMANS 12:2 reminds us, just like the changing of the clouds,
so our minds should be changing and radically so,
"DO NOT BE CONFORMED TO THIS WORLD,
but be transformed by the renewal of your mind,
that by testing you may discern what is the will of God,
what is good and acceptable and perfect."

As you are growing and changing and life is evolving around you, be
comforted to know this as HEBREWS 13:8 tells us poignantly,
"JESUS CHRIST IS THE SAME YESTERDAY,
AND TODAY, AND FOREVER."

Yes, I am thankful for the changing of the clouds and the
grace filled reminder that we will be growing too as
long as we are here and that is good and right.
Go have a beautiful day on your ever-changing journey!

Thankful Thursday #16

Today I am thankful for STAIRS!

I am thankful for stairs because they showcase a sliver (in my crazy brain anyway) of what our sanctification process may look like to the heavenly realm.

They don't move, but are available for us to make the choice which way we will move on them.

I am thankful for them because they just stay strong, patiently waiting, providing a choice with no enticement one way or the other.

Maybe sometimes I think I am making the right choice to go down the stairs, but instead have backslidden in an area I should have known better in and chosen wiser.

The good news though is that God doesn't condemn us for our bad choices and mistakes or looking back and moving backwards and then back up again. He knows that we are finite beings sometimes misunderstanding what our next step is and is there to love us anyway.

I am so thankful for the stairs being there to remind us that we really can choose to go up and keep moving forward and to keep pressing on and answer the call to go upwards!

Stairs can be long and treacherous if there is no railway to hang onto. Sometimes they can be all encompassing as if all concrete all around and no way to see in between the steps themselves.

The super cool thing about the stairs as it relates to our spiritual life is that you can never reach the top of them this side of heaven. There is always more growth to be had, more learning to be done, more love to be shown, and more people to come alongside of on this journey.

The best part about stairs is the upward part. Even though we don't get to reach the top this side of heaven, He is calling us upwards.

He is growing us with each step. The more we keep our eyes focused on the very step we are on and the one next step in front of us, the more we will enjoy this beautiful journey of life as we climb up the steps instead of worrying about what is behind us or 5 steps forward.

They are the path to our real home but we can't get there in one leap and bound. We have to take each step as it comes and learn and love on that very step until the next one comes and so on.

Yes, it's so hard sometimes when we feel as if we just slipped 5 or more steps back and can barely move ahead as we are so frustrated with our own sinfulness and humanity, but that's not how it works my friend.

SCRIPTURES FOR THE DAY

2 PETER 3:9 tells us that,
"The Lord is not slow in keeping His promise,
as some understand slowness.
INSTEAD HE IS PATIENT WITH YOU,
not wanting anyone to perish,
but everyone to come to repentance."

PHILLIPIANS 1:6 tells us,
"being confident of this,
THAT HE WHO BEGAN A GOOD WORK IN YOU
WILL CARRY IT ON TO COMPLETION
until the day of Christ Jesus."

**Let's be thankful for stairs today and the life lessons
they provide when we take out those perspective glasses
and look at them from an entirely new vantage point.**

Thankful Thursday #17

Today I am thankful for animals, specifically, OUR PETS.

I admire how simply they love and trust with no question.

These are the animals that God made in order to come alongside of us (I believe) in our lonesome times or to simply be that listening ear that doesn't judge and instead fully seems to understand our pains somehow.

It's no accident that God gave us animals. He is incapable of making mistakes. All of His creation, from the world, to the planets, to us as humans, and even the animals are a part of Him representing His glory and majesty.

So, with that being said, it should be an easy transition into why our pets are so special and how they love so unequivocally.

I am not sure in my whole life that I had a best friend quite the way I had in my dog, Barney, growing up.

Barney was a part beagle/part basset mutt long before there were ever custom mix breeds. He was THE MOST PATIENT PERFECT DOG ON THE PLANET.

I had a rough time in school getting picked on. I was that kid that just didn't understand how to fit in and was just happy to be alive and loving life. So, when I had a rough day, I would come home, call Barney to my room, or go outside and sit with him and just talk to him. He was the best listener, always let me lay my head on him if I wanted. When I got to the sad parts, he would look his sweet basset like eyes up at me like he knew and when "the talk" was over, he would cuddle me and hang around my side for quite a while after.

He never judged me, talked down to me, gave me unwanted advice. *I think God made animals not to speak to show us how important* listening *truly is.*

He was also my playmate after school as well. I think a lot about Barney even now as I am grown with my own children and he is long gone. I am thankful for all the sweet moments that he gave up running around and playing and eating or whatever just to sit and be with me. Just to sit and hear my tears and love me and be my companion.

What lessons we can learn from our pets.

Now my girls have a leopard gecko, and he is their little companion. To be honest with you, I have kind of fallen for this little guy too as he has a very gentle spirit about him. He loves to come up to us when we are near his habitat and press his little hand against the glass to ours. He will sit on our hands ever so gently. He even smiles.

His smiles speak so much to me about the simplicity of life and how we should just smile at it all.

His world is totally enough for him and you can see plainly here with this precious smile on his face that he is content and more than content, experiencing joy in his world.

Animals can teach us so much if only we would adopt their beautiful attitudes towards our world and the people in our own lives.

SCRIPTURES FOR THE DAY

JEREMIAH 8:7 tells us,
"EVEN THE STORK IN THE SKY KNOWS HER
APPOINTED SEASONS, and the dove, the swift and the
thrush observe the time of their migration. But my people
do not know the requirements of the LORD."

PROVERBS 6:6-8 even instructs us to learn from the animals!
"GO TO THE ANT, you sluggard; CONSIDER
ITS WAYS AND BE WISE!
It has no commander, no overseer or ruler, yet it stores its
provisions in summer and gathers its food at harvest."

*PROVERBS 12:10 tells us how He expects us to treat
His creatures that He made,*
"WHOEVER IS RIGHTEOUS HAS REGARD
FOR THE LIFE OF HIS BEAST,
but the mercy of the wicked is cruel."

Yes, thankful for these incredible creatures He created
for us to enjoy, take care of and love. I am thankful
that He should think so much of us as to give us love
in the form of such beautiful special creatures.

Thankful Thursday #18

Today, I am thankful for the methodical,
soul-calming, pitter-patter rhythm of RAIN!

It is a well known fact by those that know me that I am a rain lover! Yes, I was married on a rainy day, but that's not the reason I love rain so much.

Rain, to me, is like a respite. It's like a pause button on the usual business of life and the seasons. It's like God giving me complete and utter permission to slow down, retreat, and just be still.

The rhythm of the rain reminds me also that it is only temporary so I want to enjoy it while I can.

When the rain comes, I love to grab a good book or my notebook to write and just be still. Opening up the blinds and watching the rhythm of the rain falling softly against the windowpane calms and thrills my heart. Meanwhile the rain comforts me that I don't have to go anywhere right now. I don't have to answer to the world for this moment in time. The rain is falling so that I don't have to. God is watering the earth and it is good.

It also gives us a break from the incredulous heat we endure here in the deep south day in and day out for 10 months out of the year normally.

The rain is a temporary relief to the unrelenting sun and business of life.

It's rhythmic droplets from heaven. It's like God is playing drums with water and we get to rejoice from the beauty and sound of it all!

Maybe it's the introvert in me that loves that time. It feels to me like the greatest permission to be home when the world wants to call me away from it in its' usual business. It is such fun to bake and clean and craft inside during the rain. On the flip side, it is also fun to go outside and play in the rain!

Welcome the rain…rejoice in it! Know that it is only temporary, and go out and even dance in it and thank God for it!

Treasure the raindrops and the solace they provide
to your heart, mind, soul, and day.

SCRIPTURES FOR THE DAY

JOEL 2:23 reminds us,
"Be glad, people of Zion, rejoice in the LORD your God,
FOR HE HAS GIVEN YOU THE AUTUMN
RAINS BECAUSE HE IS FAITHFUL.
He sends you abundant showers,
both autumn and spring rains, as before."

and again, we are reminded of the beauty of the rain in JOB 5:10
"HE PROVIDES RAIN FOR THE EARTH;
He sends water on the countryside."

ENJOY the temporary soul relief of rain and thank God
for providing us with the water necessary for life!

Thankful Thursday #19

Today I am wildly thankful for SNOW and all the life lessons and scripture parallels it provides!

Snow…it is so quiet you can't hear it when it falls. It is so soft, but disintegrates if you touch just one piece with your hand. It is so fresh and pure yet becomes so dirty once people walk on it.

It is that one thing that is so perfectly pure, silent, soft, gentle, and white that it is unlike any other part of creation.

One reason it is so easy for me to be thankful for snow is because we live in a part of the country where that is a crazy anomaly not likely to be had. When we do get it, like a couple of years ago, it maybe as much as a 1/4 of an inch because it just doesn't snow here. This picture was taken 10 years ago when we lived in Georgia and it was the most snow we had ever seen!

I have always loved snow. From the time I was a child and got to actually see and play in some of it when visiting my northern relatives. I think the thing that fascinates me most is how it not only changes the entire topography of an area, but it seems to change the people as well.

Snow becomes like a blanket not only for the earth, but for people's souls as well.

There is something about snow that, as rain does, makes for a cozy, welcoming feeling. It can have that same effect where you want to curl up in a ball and read a good book by the fireplace.

What I notice when it snows down here in the South where people are truly fascinated by it is that we all want to come outside in it and play. We want to touch it, take pictures of it, and rejoice over it with one another.

Then I notice that of course our couple of millimeters of perfectly manicured soft layer of white on the tips of our dead grass has turned into a milky mud mess and is no longer pretty.

It gets me thinking of how life is like that right?

God made this TRULY INCREDIBLE MIND BLOWING WORLD.

Think of it like the perfect snow!

We come along and we trample all over his perfect world; messing things up, not listening to Him and what He wants us to do with it, and now it becomes a big milky mud mess.

The good news is though that He is gracious. He wants us to play in His creation, so don't be discouraged thinking you shouldn't play in the snow…that's not the message at all! I won't ever stop playing in the snow that's for sure!

*The message is simply that each day and really each moment
is like a new layer of perfectly white snow God gives us
because He really does love us THAT MUCH!*

SCRIPTURES FOR THE DAY

PSALM 51:7 paints a lovely picture,
**"Purify me with hyssop, and I shall be clean; WASH
ME, AND I SHALL BE WHITER THAN SNOW."**

*It's no wonder we are supposed to be in awe of snow as
MATTHEW 28:3 shows us even snow points us to Jesus,*
**"His appearance was like lightning, and
HIS CLOTHES WERE WHITE AS SNOW!"**

**YES, today I am thankful for the wondrous gift
of snow and how it points us to the purity of our
Risen Savior and His mercies towards us.**

Thankful Thursday #20

Today I am thankful for the CROSS.

*Yes, the one that held my dear precious Savior nailed to it
to suffer the vilest death completely undeserved.*

I am grateful and thankful for something so despicable, so ugly, so offensive and vile that ended up becoming a beautiful symbol of love.

In this day and age we tend to pretty up the cross and make it this sparkly little gold or diamond pendant we wear as a necklace or bracelet to symbolize our faith. And there's nothing wrong with that, but hang with me for a minute here.

I am here to tell you *that cross* was known as the most despicable, humiliating, dehumanizing way to die back then. It was reserved for the lowest of the lowest.

But, that cross…oh the tormenting agony of how thankful I am for it and my Savior who chose to stay up there and undeservedly take my wrath so that I could have hope to be with Him forever and be forgiven.

It is good and right to be thankful for things that are ugly and offensive when they point to something far greater, more beautiful, and powerful that makes the gratitude make sense after all!

Make no mistake either that God picked that way for His Son to die His earthly death. He chose the cross for so many reasons.

As He carried that heavy, torturous cross, he symbolized carrying the weight of our heinous sins and that He was willing to do that for you and for me!

The cross held his precious dying mutilated body up for everyone to see. There would be no denying what was happening. He also chose to do it right alongside 2 other people that He wanted to be with and comfort them in their last hour. In all of this He wanted you and me to know that *He chose this because He chooses US!!!*

So, knowing all of this, how can I not be thankful for the cross as torturous as that gratitude may feel.

SCRIPTURES FOR THE DAY

HEBREWS 12:28 boldly reminds us why we are to have hearts of gratitude!
"Therefore, since WE ARE RECEIVING A KINGDOM THAT
CANNOT BE SHAKEN, LET US BE THANKFUL,
and so worship God acceptably with reverence and awe,"

*COLOSSIANS 2:14 gives us the exact reason we are
to be thankful for the cross,*
"HAVING CANCELLED THE CHARGE
of our legal indebtedness,
WHICH STOOD AGAINST US
and condemned us; he has taken it away,
NAILING IT TO THE CROSS."

I mean, come on...really? How could we NOT be
thankful for that? There is always, always, always
something to be thankful for my friend!

Be thankful for the cross today! It offers us HOPE!

Thankful Thursday #21

Today, I am beyond thankful for
ALL OF OUR DIFFERENCES!

Probably one of the best lessons I have learned since we moved to the big city is the beauty and necessity of our differences. It takes all types of people to make the world make sense and to display God's never-ending beauty and mercies.

I have so many friends that are so the opposite of me in so many ways whether it be by simple things like age or sex or location of where we live, or by deeper things...our history, our struggles, our viewpoints on life, and so much more.

I am so grateful that God allowed us to live in a big city so that I could learn just how big and wonderful the world truly is! He didn't make just one type of person and there is no such thing as one type being better than another. Sorry Joneses…not trying to keep up with you here, nor are you the end game!

We don't even need specific Bible verses to back this up, although I will get to that.

Simply look at scripture and the entirety of it and the world around you.

God could have very simply made all of who He wanted into 2 people… Adam and Eve and let them be, grow old, eventually die, and that be it.

But He didn't.

In the Bible, there are all types of people from bold brave warriors like David to the quiet seemingly insecure types like Esther that God used in mighty ways. He has wired us each differently to accomplish different jobs for His Kingdom.

Our differences matter and should be celebrated. I love that so many of my friends and their lives look nothing like my own because that means I can learn so much from them! I am thankful they allow me to be a part of their life as I am also different from them as well.

I love to humbly ask people that are so different from me how they do certain things that I admire or how they learned to do a certain thing. It keeps my eyes and ears and heart open to love fully right now where I am and hopefully be a light for Jesus.

Let's stop berating others for their differences and instead rejoice that we are all image bearers of Christ and that there is great beauty in that. What can we learn from one another?

God obviously doesn't have just one facet to Him; otherwise there would have been one person with one trait. If we are image bearers (and we are), and He keeps on making people that are so wildly different with different interests, talents, and gifts, then all that should do is draw us towards those other people to learn more about Christ!

None of us are better than the other...we are all equally important...there is no ultimate goal of one life winning it all. The beauty lies in our differences!

SCRIPTURES FOR THE DAY

GALATIANS 3:28 tells us there is not one better than another,
**"There is neither Jew nor Greek, there is neither slave
nor free, there is no male and female, for
YOU ARE ALL ONE IN CHRIST JESUS."**

I PETER 3:8 reminds us how we are to behave towards each other,
**"Finally, all of you, be like-minded,
BE SYMPATHETIC, LOVE ONE ANOTHER,
be compassionate and humble."**

*JOHN 13:34-35 reminds us why we should want to
love everyone regardless of our differences,*
**"A new commandment I give to you, that
YOU LOVE ONE ANOTHER; JUST AS I HAVE LOVED YOU,
you also are to love one another. By this all people will know
that you are my disciples, if you have love for one another."**

**Let's be thankful how unique and special we all are and
focus on the beauty of that and grow from it accordingly!**

Thankful Thursday #22

Today I am ever so grateful for THE VALLEYS.

Yes, those dark deep trenches where all you can see on all sides is seemingly impassable mountains with no light piercing the darkness.

I know that is deep…deep and painful, so bare with me here.

Why in the world you may be thinking would I be thankful for the dark deep valleys.

Here is why.

Because we can recognize it is a valley.

Wait…steep in that for just a moment.

If all of life was a valley and it was darkness all the time, would we even know it is a valley? How could we? There is no possible way we would know.

We have to have the contrast of the mountaintops to even recognize that it is a valley.

So why be thankful for the valleys? Because usually that is where the lessons are learned, where fortitude is built, where full and complete surrender happens, and where you become nothing so that God can fill you with His everything.

It's not a pretty place. I don't want to go back there. I hate it for my husband and children and friends that knew me when I was in that dark deep valley that I saw no way out of.

It wasn't building grit or fortitude at the time, but it emptied me completely…of everything.

I used to often wonder "why" when I was in the valley or even be angry at God for all the trials I had walked through and even misunderstood the point of the valley and began to think God hated me. I couldn't have been more wrong.

As it turns out, what I have learned is that a faith that hasn't been tested, is a faith that shouldn't be trusted.

It was then that I learned that until we are emptied of it all, He can't fill us up with what He wants for us.

I want to know that the trials and valleys were the key that God used to unlock the beauty that I didn't know lied within, and to see that beauty in others all around me.

We all have stuff, right? It's not up to us to play the compare or shame game or my stuff is harder or better than yours. All that does is damage the person going through their valley.

The valleys or trials can do one of 2 things, and I hope for you like it turned out for me eventually that it becomes the latter.

They can either harden your heart, become your whole identity, and make you bitter and angry.

OR

They can humble you. They can soften your heart, reveal your true identity in Christ, and produce a thankful heart with eyes to see.

The Valleys are quite often the road to the biggest blessings around. I am not referring to monetary or physical blessings this side of heaven though, so let's make that clear.

I am referring to the much more real, life changing blessings of having eyes to see the hurting, a heart that can come alongside those hurting and hands that long to serve.

The valleys in this life can be the biggest blessings as God can use them to change our paradigm for His glory.

I don't know about you, but I don't want to be a bitter, hardened heart that identifies my entire being with the valleys.

Today as hard as it hurts, I am thankful for the valleys, hard stuff, and trials in this life as they draw me closer and closer to my true home and soften my heart to shower others with His love.

I know that it's not fun. I know that it can plain suck. But, I do know, the valley is JUST THAT…a valley…NOT your forever!

So rejoice that the valley is recognizable and that you can trust there are mountaintops in your future. Rejoice that it helps you know the difference in a valley and a mountaintop and therefore gives hope!

And we know that hope never disappoints!

SCRIPTURES FOR THE DAY

PSALM 23:4 JUST STRUCK ME IN A BRAND NEW WAY!
Check this out..
"Even though I WALK THROUGH THE VALLEY
of the shadow of death, I fear no evil, for You are with
me; Your rod and Your staff, they comfort me."

Did you *see* that?
Even in the valley we are MOVING…we are walking
THROUGH it! It's not a stagnant place.
It's a PLACE OF MOVEMENT on towards greater and better things!

We are not being torn down, but being built up with character!
Look at THIS BEAUTIFUL VERSE THAT PROVES IT!

ROMANS 5:3-5 tells us of our hope through trials,
"Not only so, but we also glory in our sufferings,
because we know that SUFFERING PRODUCES
PERSEVERANCE; PERSEVERANCE, CHARACTER;
AND CHARACTER, HOPE. AND HOPE
DOES NOT PUT US TO SHAME,
because God's love has been poured out into our hearts
through the Holy Spirit, who has been given to us."

The valley is only temporary my friend. We can be thankful
for that, and that we have those valleys to show us that
there is something else to hope for in the mountaintop!

Thankful Thursday #23

Today I am thankful for ROOFTOPS and the covering and protection they provide.

I believe they can be something our culture takes for granted. Maybe we hardly even notice them unless they're leaking.

They are the unnoticed tops of the buildings and homes that provide us our everyday work and living space.

Do we ever thank God for there being a place we can duck into to get out of the heat, rain, snow, or wind?

Without a rooftop, awning, or covering what good would a building be? It would only be walls with nothing connecting them overhead. There would be no protection from the elements, no safety from the outside world.

That's so much like Jesus for me. What about you?

He is my rooftop, my awning, my safe covering and without Him, all my walls don't matter because He is what covers it all, holds it all together, and provides me with safety from the world.

SCRIPTURES FOR THE DAY

PSALM 59:1 is a powerful and comforting description,
"Deliver me from my enemies, O God;
BE MY FORTRESS against those
who are attacking me."

while

PSALM 91:4 reminds us beautifully,
"HE WILL COVER YOU with His feathers,
and under His wings you will find refuge;
His faithfulness will be your shield and rampart."

I am so thankful for the rooftops, awnings, and
coverings of buildings and the spiritual picture
they lend to point to our Heavenly Father.

I am thankful how He so graciously covers
us with His protection and is always there
regardless if we notice Him or not.

Thankful Thursday #24

Today I am thankful for DOORWAYS!

I love knowing something, as I think most of us do. I love knowing there is a way in and a way out…do you know what I mean here?

Today I am thankful for that tangible representation of the way in and out in our physical world.

Sometimes we just need to know there is a way in. We need to know we are welcome and will always have a place at the table so to speak. We will always be welcome no matter the time that passes since we have visited. We aren't rejected or uninvited and can come in and be a part of the festivities. It's a warm massage to the soul knowing we have a way in.

Sometimes it's needing to know there is a way out. Whether it is in the physical sense like at a party or ballgame or concert, or whether in the spiritual realm like an abusive relationship, long-suffering trials of caring for a sick relative, or any other type of trial. It's so comforting to know there is always a safe escape.

I'm thankful for the spiritual reality that God is our doorway and I'm thankful that he gives us doorways in our physical world to represent the entering of His Word and His kingdom as well.

What happens when we cross through a doorway? We have made a distinct difference in where our physical presence is, right? If I go to the gym from the parking lot, I am now in that place and know what to do there. I know what is expected of me and what will happen in the general sense.

What about when we desperately need a way out and emergency call button if you will and there is no doorway and we are in real trouble?

God is our doorway, and He won't ever disappoint, fail to be there or have the door locked. He is always ready for us to cross through and be there with Him. He has the best open door policy ever!

SCRIPTURES FOR THE DAY

MATTHEW 7:7 reminds us,
"Continue to ask, and God will give to you.
Continue to search, and you will find.
Continue to knock, and
THE DOOR WILL OPEN FOR YOU."

REVELATION 3:8 gives the little girl inside of me
goosebumps of safety and comfort all over my soul,
"I know all the things you do, and
I HAVE OPENED A DOOR FOR YOU
THAT NO ONE CAN CLOSE.
You have little strength, yet you
obeyed my word and did not deny me."

Next time you pass through a doorway,
ponder on Revelation 3:8 and His loving arms
holding the door wide open for you.

Let's find gratitude in our hearts and souls for
doorways and the promise they provide!

Thankful Thursday #25

Today I am thankful for FOOTPRINTS.

Footprints are a visual, tangible encouragement to press forward because no matter what is going on in our lives or what path we are on, WE ARE NOT ALONE!

There is a changing of attitude and movement that happens when you *believe* you can do something. Part of that belief has to come from *knowing* that no matter how it may seem in this physical world, you are not alone. Someone has gone before you. Someone will go after you. But for now, in this moment, *it is your turn.* You must press on and move forward.

One of my absolute favorite things to do when I was temporarily living in my car before I went in to work for the day was to walk on the beach. I would look around for the footprints and I would be so motivated and inspired to keep going.

> *Those footsteps whispered to me, "All this is is ONE STEP! That's it! This is NOT YOUR FOREVER! You can do this! Others have been through stuff before you and will go through stuff after you. All you need to do is press on."*

They are a physical real-world reminder of what God is whispering to our souls all throughout the day whether or not we hear it..."I am with you and after I will make a way for you! I will carry you. I will be in front of you, behind you, and all around you! I will make a way for you!" (*Look at Genesis 28:15*)

Footprints also represent faith. We are told that faith is the assurance of things hoped for and not seen. So with footprints, we sometimes don't get to see the person that made those footprints. We don't get to ask them how they did it or for suggestions. We just have to go on faith that they were there, trekked their own path and we can do it too.

Footprints are all about knowing we are not alone and stepping out in faith! They are the visual imprint of forward momentum. I love to imagine the footprint I see is that of my Heavenly Father and it is His message to me saying, "I've got you. I won't ever abandon you. I have gone before you and am all around you."

SCRIPTURES FOR THE DAY

*PHILIPPIANS 3:12-14 boldly tells us of the forward
movement we are to be making,*
"Not that I have already obtained this or am already perfect, but
I PRESS ON TO MAKE IT MY OWN,
because Christ Jesus has made me His own.
Brothers, I do not consider that I have made it my own.
But one thing I do: forgetting what lies behind and
STRAINING FORWARD to what lies ahead,
I PRESS ON TOWARD THE GOAL for the prize
of the upward call of God in Christ Jesus."

2 Corinthians 5:7 reminds us how we are to be making footprints,
"For WE WALK BY FAITH, not by sight."

**YES, today I am thankful for footprints and our
loving Heavenly Father who gives them to us to
be a beautiful reminder that we are not alone!**

Thankful Thursday #26

Today I am thankful for SEA TURTLE RELEASES.

I am particularly thankful for how they flap their front flippers when they are being released back into the wild after having been rehabbed.

This is something very personal for me and I sobbed big crocodile mourning tears as I learned about this particular thing I am so thankful for.

We recently had the honor of attending an adult sea turtle release. These turtles had been rescued when caught in fishing lines, or other traumatic circumstances, rehabbed for months and were checked off officially healthy enough to go back and live where they are meant to…in the wild.

Thankfully, there was an opening on the very front near the water's edge. Our family excitedly took our place there to watch the releases. I couldn't help but notice something very distinct time after time. As the workers holding these large mammoth turtles got within about 5 feet of the water line…they would begin to wildly flap their flippers.

OK…now I am crying…I will explain why.

I finally got the chance to ask one rehabber…are they doing that because they can sense they are close to going home?

> She smiled and replied "That is EXACTLY WHY THEY DO IT."
> She said "If you notice when they are in the truck getting out of the
> crate they are docile and still. As we carry them over the sand they
> are noticeably unchanged. But as we approach the water line and
> they hear the waves calling to them and they know they are going
> home where they belong, they begin to get very excited and come alive
> and flap wildly. This is also an indication they are truly ready!"

I began to sob.

I immediately thought of my mom after nearly 10 years to the day living completely trapped in her own body as a C1 quadriplegic. I painfully recalled seeing her in her last days and how lifeless and in pain and miserable she was.

I imagined her in her last moments flapping her spiritual wings crying out from her soul to Jesus, "Yes Jesus Yes! Please Take Me Home WHERE I REALLY BELONG." And my heart could bear it no more…I was overcome on the beach watching these incredible creatures knowing full well where they belong and coming alive at the very sound of knowing home was within reach.

I have to imagine my mom so happy to be free from the confines of that wheelchair and that body that was permanently stopped from any movement, no matter what she willed or wanted to do.

Oh, I long to be like the sea turtles when I worship or just think about Jesus or just fellowship with others…flapping my spiritual wings knowing I am in His presence.

SCRIPTURE FOR THE DAY

It's like somehow they know this from 1 CORINTHIANS 15:51-57,
"Behold! I TELL YOU A MYSTERY.
We shall not all sleep, but WE SHALL ALL BE CHANGED,
in a moment, in the twinkling of an eye, at the last trumpet.
For the trumpet will sound, and the dead will be raised
imperishable, and WE SHALL BE CHANGED.
For this perishable body must put on the imperishable, and this
mortal body must put on immortality. When the perishable
puts on the imperishable, and the mortal puts on immortality,
then shall come to pass the saying that is written:
"DEATH IS SWALLOWED UP IN VICTORY."
"O death, where is your victory? O death, where is your sting?""

Flap away sweet sea turtles as you head home.
I am so thankful for your witness to me in how I
should worship and look forward to everyday life!

Thankful Thursday #27

Today I am thankful for the
"once-in-a-lifetime" gift of TODAY!

Too often we get sucked into dealing with all the pressures of today, tomorrow, and beyond. It becomes all about the planning and getting ready and meeting deadlines and well, you name it.

No more!

Listen friend, you and I…we are NOT promised tomorrow. I could be gone tomorrow. I have to live today as if I really believe that, with all the cells in my being. Not from a worried sad perspective, but from an over joyous, dumbfounded at the gift of today vantage point!

All that calls us to do today is to be present and grateful for this day as it is what we have been given; until and if the next one comes.

If I could impress upon you things to do with this day, it would be to seek beauty everywhere, be grateful, and to speak kindness and truth with great love.

I am a passionate person by nature because I have seen and experienced so much which makes me highly aware that at any moment every single bit of it could be gone with no warning. I want to know that I did all I could to love everyone in my life the best I could and with no holds barred.

Live as if everything could go away because it really could, *but be joyous that it is here now.*

We were all born, and will all eventually die, but right now right here today is a wildly crazy gift that we can't give back, do over, or get again.

That day you have been waiting for, looking for, hanging on until just the right time? There is no perfect day or timing. This is it my friend! THIS IS THE DAY YOU HAVE BEEN GIVEN! What will you do with it?

> *You are here for such a time as this! Just imagine that little orphan girl Esther who had no idea God was going to use what she saw as an ordinary life and day and use it for His greatness.*

SCRIPTURES FOR THE DAY

JAMES 4:13-14 reminds us not to get sucked into all
the pressures and planning of the day,
"Come now, you who say, "TODAY OR TOMORROW
WE WILL GO into such and such a town and spend
a year there and trade and make a profit"— yet
YOU DO NOT KNOW WHAT TOMORROW MAY BRING.
What is your life?
For you are a mist that appears for a little
time and then vanishes."

Even looking to the Lord's Prayer and the very specific
way we are taught to pray, MATTHEW 6:11,
"Give us THIS DAY our daily bread,"

PSALM 118:24 even tells us what our attitudes
and actions for today should look like,
"THIS IS THE DAY that the Lord has made; let
us REJOICE AND BE GLAD IN IT."

Yes, let's be grateful and even joyous for this
wildly amazing gift called TODAY!

Thankful Thursday #28

Today I am thankful for TATTOOS.

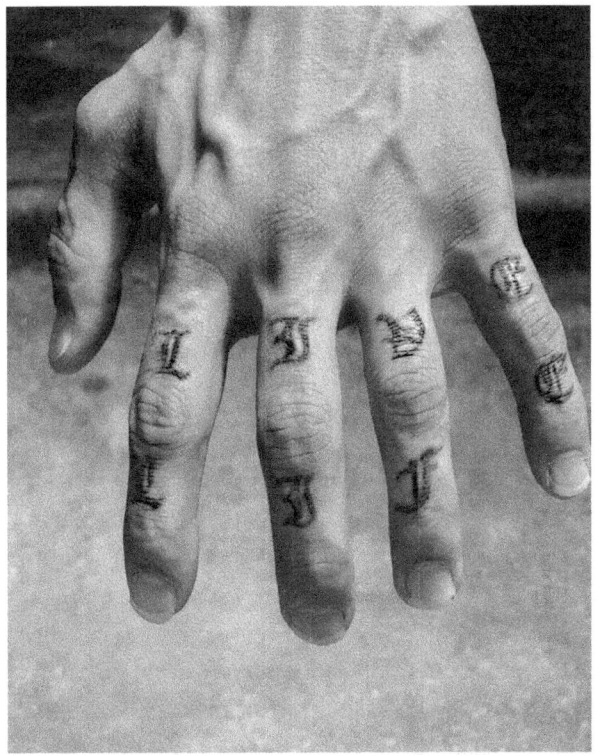

Today I am thankful for something that for some reason some people don't understand.

I love finding things to be thankful for that some people may see as weird or controversial, but I see as beautiful through a heavenly lens.

For those of you that know me in real life you may think well why are you thankful for those when you don't even have any? That's a great question and here is the answer.

There are plenty of writings and opinions on whether or not tattoos are biblical or not. So many times we like to get so sucked into thinking we have all the answers for every situation or question. That perspective, in the past has honestly sucked the life and joy out of me.

Here is my perspective. I have decided to seek out beauty and be grateful for *everything* around me, no matter what someone's opinion is on it. Remember this is about perspective and opening our eyes.

Where others see controversy, I see an open soul.

I personally am thankful for them and the lessons they provide and what they point us towards! I have always been drawn to them, intrigued by them, and find great beauty lies within them.

It is like having a window into a piece of that person's soul without ever even talking to them. It's humbling to be in the midst of that level of openness. They are bold enough to be transparent with their innermost pain, and greatest joys and share it with the world...what an awe inspiring way to live life!

Here is what I find so beautiful about tattoos...it's the being bold enough to engrave and show on the outside what must so passionately lie on the inside. It's being willing to go through the painful process of getting the tattoo in order to make it a permanent part of who that person is.

THAT IS EXACTLY WHAT JESUS DID FOR US!

He was willing to go through the painful process of torture just to make us His own permanently! And He proclaims from everywhere that we are His.

How can I not be thankful for that?

Just because I don't have one doesn't mean I can't appreciate and be thankful for what they represent and point me towards.

It also points to a greater tattoo of sorts that I love to think about.

See the 1st verse below from Isaiah!

SCRIPTURES FOR THE DAY

*ISAIAH 49:16 gives me great comfort during times
of trials, betrayal, or feeling forgotten.*
**"Behold, I have ENGRAVED YOU ON THE PALMS
OF MY HANDS."**

*1 PETER 1:18-19 describes just how much He was willing
to go through and give up to make you His,*
**"Knowing that YOU WERE RANSOMED from the futile ways
inherited from your forefathers, NOT WITH PERISHABLE
THINGS such as silver or gold, BUT WITH THE PRECIOUS
BLOOD OF CHRIST, like that of a lamb without blemish or spot."**

**Wow…just wow…is it any wonder
I am thankful for tattoos?**

**Yes, today I am thankful for tattoos. Anytime I see
one, it reminds me that Jesus went through the
painful process to make me His and has my name
engraved on His hand and He cannot forget me.**

Thankful Thursday #29

Today I am thankful for
OLD DILAPIDATED BUILDINGS
that someone saves and gives new life!

Today I am so very thankful for something that most people pass by and don't notice at all. If they do notice it they may make comments that it should be destroyed or leveled.

Too often we see old buildings, if we see them at all, and think someone should demolish it. The problem with this thinking is that it focuses solely on the exterior physical appearance and can carry over to how we view other things in life, even people.

If we see a homeless person on the side of the road, do we also think, "oh they should be carried off somewhere and put away?"

No! Certainly not! Or at least I hope that's nobody's thoughts.

Think of those lucky old buildings that someone sees the beauty in. Instead of destroying it, they fix it up, save the structure, shore it up, and make it as strong as ever. They spend time caring for it and give it a new life on the inside.

Well, that's really what God does for us.
We are this dilapidated old building of sorts that really is torn
down, battered, beaten up and nothing to offer, but GOD!

Then He comes along, saves us, shores us up with armor and
beautifies us on the inside and out and gives us a brand new life.

I am thankful that God is the architect that sees me (the old building) as worth saving and investing His time and resources in, so that maybe I can offer some light to the world while I'm still here!

SCRIPTURES FOR THE DAY

PSALM 147:3 tells us He does see, love, and fix the broken ones,
"He HEALS the brokenhearted and BINDS UP THEIR WOUNDS."

1 PETER 5:10 lovingly describes the restoration process,
"And the God of all grace, who called you to His eternal
glory in Christ, after you have suffered a little while,
WILL HIMSELF RESTORE YOU AND MAKE YOU
STRONG, FIRM, AND STEADFAST."

Another beautiful reminder is found in 2 CORINTHIANS 4:16-17,
"Therefore we do not lose heart.
Though OUTWARDLY WE ARE WASTING AWAY,
yet inwardly we are BEING RENEWED DAY BY DAY.
For our light and momentary troubles are achieving for
us an eternal glory that far outweighs them all."

**Oh yes, I love an old fixer upper of a building because
it points me every time to Christ and how He
chooses to save us and fix us up better than new!**

Thankful Thursday #30

Today I am thankful for ONE WAY SIGNS!

This Thankful Thursday we are getting back to basics.

Today I am thankful for something we see everyday and while we obey it and do what it says (otherwise there would be multiple wrecks) we tend to lose sight of it when it comes to our spiritual lives.

They are a humble reminder in this physical world that there really is only ONE WAY to Heaven in the spiritual world and we tend to forget that.

Or maybe I am alone in that?

We tend to think, "Oh here's something I could DO God, or here's someone I helped God, or how about looking at things this way God?"

The answer is "No, no, and a resounding no."

We could never DO enough to earn our way to Heaven.

We can't look at things our way and think we can figure Him out better than He knows Himself and us.

We can't be pretty enough, work hard enough, or serve enough to enter the Kingdom of Heaven.

SCRIPTURES FOR THE DAY

EPHESIANS 2:8-9 tells us we can't earn our way there,
"For by grace you have been saved through faith.
And this is NOT YOUR OWN DOING;
it is the gift of God, NOT A RESULT OF WORKS,
so that no one may boast."
so...that is the wrong way to try.

JOHN 14:6 tells us the ONE WAY,
"Jesus said to him, "I AM THE WAY,
and The Truth,
and The Life.
NO ONE COMES TO THE FATHER EXCEPT THROUGH ME."

I am thankful for the ONE WAY signs and how they
point to Jesus and remind me to keep it simple silly!

Thankful Thursday #31

Today I am crazy thankful for DANCING!

This one is about freedom, joy, worship, movement and expression rolled into one!

Dancing is the outward expression of the cells of my soul laughing and my heart overflowing with joy. Dancing spills out!

It's what happens when you can no longer contain the joy inside!

Dancing is freedom...fully expressing yourself in a way that is understood by some and misunderstood by others.

Either way it matters not.

Dancing is another language. There are so many different styles of dance. Each one has its own beauty, rhythm, meaning, intention, and style.

It's a language that should be welcomed as expressing the passion of the soul.

Dancing is becoming like a kid again and not caring what others think when you let your body free to dance joyfully to express your gratitude of joy for life!

Those that know me know I love to dance! I didn't say I am good at it or can do it well, but when the music kicks in and the beat is familiar...it's literally like I can't help myself! Can't stop, won't stop! It's being fully free to be the real me and express my inner joy!

Why would God give us music and rhythm if He didn't want us to dance?

We don't have to have perfect rhythm or the right steps or moves. Just be free, let loose, and experience the unbridled joy that dancing brings!

It takes boldness to be fully you and step out and care not what others or the world are thinking. Let go, be fully you...let your inner joy spill out into the physical realm of dancing!

SCRIPTURE PROOF WE SHOULD DANCE!

PSALM 149:3 even tells us to dance!
"Let them PRAISE HIS NAME WITH DANCING;
Let them sing praises to Him with timbrel and lyre."

2 SAMUEL 6:14a paints a powerful picture!
"And David DANCED BEFORE THE LORD
with all his might."

PSALM 30:11a even tells us He has given it to us
as a reprieve from suffering,
"You have turned for me MY MOURNING INTO DANCING;"

Yes, today let's be thankful for dancing and the soulful expression it provides to pour out the joy that can no longer be contained inside!

Thankful Thursday #32

Today I am crazy thankful for EXERCISE!

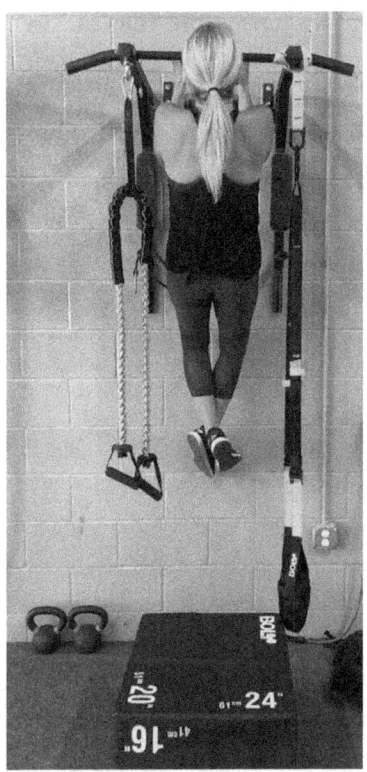

This day I am thankful for something that I also use as a method of thanksgiving to God.

I am so very thankful that for this moment in time God allows my body to move so I will USE IT to move and be strong and glorify Him as long as He allows!

Watching my mom be unable to move at all no matter what for the last 10 years of her life had a profound impact on me and my deep understanding of *having the ability to move.*

It doesn't mean it's not painful or that it's not hard. *Simply BEING ABLE* to move. I have 2 shredded knees, 1 torn shoulder, and multiple other injuries and issues, but I am still CAPABLE of movement whether it hurts or not.

Our bodies are a once-in-a-lifetime gift! They aren't supposed to all look the same so get out of your head that this is about some ideal image. It simply isn't! This is about something so much more profound!

We are supposed to work hard with our hands and exercise our body as well as our mind as a thankfulness to God that He allows us to move!

Exercise is not just about our bodies...even physical exercise...it clears the cobwebs in our minds and hearts. It gets the blood flowing, heart racing, and mind believing that we are able!

It is a celebration of what YOUR BODY CAN DO!

Exercise quite literally saved my sanity and my life multiple times in my life when I was empty and broken. Enter stage right exercise to get the movement, offering, and sacrifice happening.

This past year as I have been exercising with more intention, I have had many people approach me and ask me why I exercise. I tell them as I point to my head that I exercise to fight the battles up here that threaten to pull me down. I also work hard exercising as a way of honoring the fight of others who literally can't exercise right now for various reasons.

Don't be deceived into thinking physical exercise is ONLY about or for the body. That is only partly the case. Physical exercise is just as necessary for our mental health as well. It's a part of the fight!

SCRIPTURES FOR THE DAY

ROMANS 12:1 paints a beautiful picture for us,
"Therefore, I urge you, brothers and sisters, in view of God's mercy, to
OFFER YOUR BODIES AS A LIVING SACRIFICE,
holy and pleasing to God—
THIS IS your true and proper WORSHIP."

Exercise should be a full-on out surrender of it all to God. It's
supposed to be hard and soul digging. It's an offering up.

It can be a hard pill to swallow and make you face
insecurities and issues you don't want to deal with, but
it becomes a literal fight and fight you shall!

1 CORINTHIANS 6:9-10 reminds us that this fight is real because
our bodies are not even our own…they are on loan…
"**Do you not know that**
YOUR BODIES ARE TEMPLES OF THE HOLY SPIRIT,
who is in you, whom you have received from God?
YOU ARE NOT YOUR OWN;
you were bought at a price.
Therefore HONOR GOD WITH YOUR BODIES."

It's OK if you are out of shape, don't know where to start, have injuries, are
fighting mental or spiritual battles right now.

You don't need to be in a good place to start.

Just simply start somewhere.

Start by going on a walk outside. Make the walk longer each day. Add in jumping jacks. Experience all the amazing things that God allows your body the strength to do, no matter how seemingly small it may seem.

He will build you up and make you stronger, mentally and spiritually, as you go along!

Since we do not know what tomorrow may bring and only have today, exercise simply because YOU CAN (*meaning have the ability to*). Don't do it because you desire to or even have a goal, but simply as a thanksgiving to God because you have been given the ability to do so today.

Thankful Thursday #33

Today I am thankful for MICROSCOPES
because they remind us to look deeper.

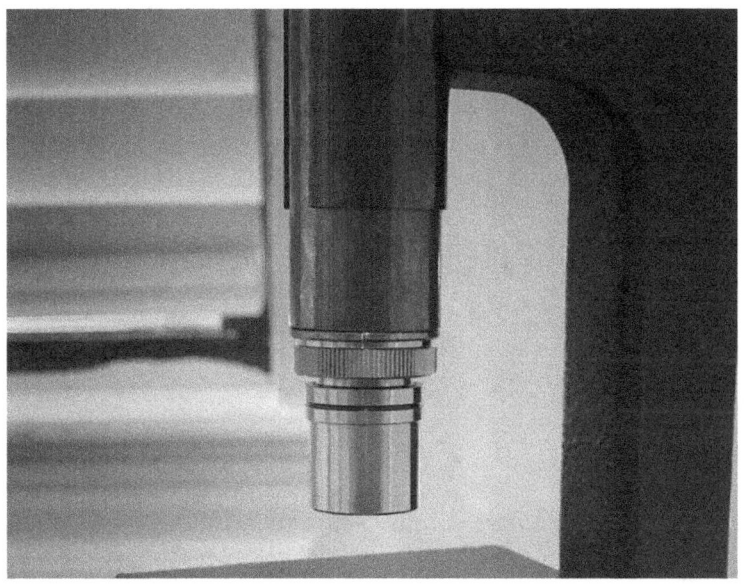

Today we are digging deeper…where we find the real beauty and meaning.

I personally LOVE to research and discover new things. I guess you could call it a hobby of mine. I find it utterly incomprehensible and fascinating how much there is to learn, discover, and uncover in life! I truly believe it's the same way with people as well! And, since we are always growing and changing, the looking deeper never really has an end!

How exciting!

> *We are called to be like Jesus and one major quality of Jesus is that*
> *He doesn't look as man looks on the surface...no in fact,*
> *God looks IN THE DEPTHS.*

Surface lookers never actually find anything...think about it...what do they see? They see what everyone sees...they discover nothing new. They know nothing of beauty in the depths. What's under that top layer?

I am so thankful for tools like microscopes and magnifying glasses that can give us a small picture into what it is like to peer and dig deeper. Dig under the surface...see what else lingers there. For at its core is its reality. Whatever the "IT" is my friend will be revealed by peering much deeper.

SCRIPTURES FOR THE DAY

PSALM 139:15 tells us,
"My frame was not hidden from you when I
was made in the secret place, when
I WAS WOVEN TOGETHER
IN THE DEPTHS OF THE EARTH."

CORINTHIANS 2:9-10 reminds us of the deeper perspective that matters,
"However, as it is written:
"What no eye has seen, what no ear has heard, and
WHAT NO HUMAN MIND HAS CONCEIVED"—
the things God has prepared for those who love Him—
these are the things GOD HAS REVEALED TO US
BY HIS SPIRIT.
The Spirit searches all things, even
THE DEEP THINGS OF GOD."

Today, let's be thankful for the deep perspective
microscopes and magnifying glasses can provide to remind
us not to stop at the surface, but to be depth seekers.

Thankful Thursday #34

Today I am thankful for TRASHCANS.

Say what?

Today I am thankful for an everyday thing that most people would view as gross or definitely not something to be thankful for at all.

> *That's right...I am thankful for trashcans and the*
> *heavenly perspective it reminds me to focus on.*

How often do we even think about trashcans and what the world would look like without them? We have a place to put our smelly, used up, unnecessary, and unwanted stuff in the world. Then we have beautiful servant hearts who are willing to come take all that nasty stuff and place it in their dumpster truck and haul it away so the trash doesn't overflow onto the streets. Once it is in the trashcan, we no longer think about it and don't want to see it again or be burdened with it.

Isn't that so much like what The Bible tells us to do and what Jesus does for us?

> *Just as trashcans are a visual reminder in this physical world of*
> *where to put our garbage and trash, so God's word tells us what to*
> *do with our bad thoughts or trash coming into to our lives.*

We are told to take every thought captive. We are all human and sinners so we are going to have bad thoughts but it's what we do with those that matters.

1. **Notice that thought.**
2. **Say "heck no" to it.**
3. **Put it in the proverbial trashcan and be done with it!**

SCRIPTURES FOR THE DAY

*CORINTHIANS 10:4-5 reminds us of the power we have
been given over the strongholds and thoughts,*
**"The weapons we fight with are not the weapons
of the world. On the contrary, they have
DIVINE POWER TO DEMOLISH STRONGHOLDS.
We demolish arguments and every pretension that sets
itself up against the knowledge of God, and we
TAKE CAPTIVE EVERY THOUGHT
to make it obedient to Christ."**

I am also thankful that the collection of our spiritual trash gets put in a dumpster that then somehow evaporates in the heavenly realm. How do I know this?

Because He promises us this in PSALM 103:12,
**"as far as the east is from the west,
SO FAR HE HAS REMOVED
OUR TRANSGRESSIONS FROM US."**

**Yes, I am very thankful for trashcans and
the beautiful reminder they give us that we
don't have to hold onto all of our junk!**

Capture it, trash it, confess it, and move forward!

Thankful Thursday #35

Today I am thankful for NATURE!

Today I am thankful for something that we may too often take for granted and yet it is the very thing we live on and in and around every day!

Yes, just absolutely all of NATURE.

From the beaches and forests, fields and deserts, to the mountaintops and anything in between.

Nature is so amazing because it reminds us of God's great love for us. He made this place JUST FOR US to have a place to live and to display His majesty to us.

He made all of this just so that we would be without excuse as He clearly displays Himself and His majesty in nature and we would have a place to live and have something to enjoy while we are here.

How crazy awesome is that? The water that gives us fish to eat, water for drinking and bathing, and so much more.

The grass that absorbs the rain waters so that it's not constantly flooding when it does rain.

The soil underneath the grass that allows the grass, flowers, and plants to grow. The trees that process carbon dioxide and gives us back oxygen which is necessary for life!

God designed and provided every single bit of it FOR US!

It also reminds us of His incredible scope of imagination just the same as He has with creating people. The nature that He has created worldwide is like nothing any of us could have fathomed up if we had our entire lives to ponder it!

When I have a hard time seeing the gratitude for something I am around every day I often like to contrast it with a "what if" in my mind that all of the sudden opens up my heart to great gratitude!

It's a mindset of contrast that brings me back to a gratitude perspective. So, let's play the "what if" game with nature.

What if God had made us all to live in concrete buildings with concrete sidewalks and we survived like that? No trees, no grass, no mountains. Well, if He had done that then that would have been perfect, because He is perfect.

Thankfully He chose otherwise.

So, when we are tempted to take the everyday beauty of nature for granted because we pass by it so often, just imagine what if nature was never here. What if you never got to see those spring flowers bloom or have a grassy yard to lie down in and watch the clouds go by? What if there were no lakes to learn to fish and swim in? No trees to give us oxygen.

Sometimes the "what if" mindset can bring us back to a full heart of gratitude for the things we may pass by everyday without a second glance.

SCRIPTURES FOR THE DAY

I TIMOTHY 4:4 even instructs us to be grateful for His creation,
"For EVERYTHING CREATED BY GOD IS GOOD, and
nothing is to be rejected if it is received with THANKSGIVING,"

ROMANS 1:20 even tells us nature is part of His witness to us,
"For since THE CREATION OF THE WORLD
God's invisible qualities—his eternal power and
divine nature—have been CLEARLY SEEN,
being understood FROM WHAT HAS BEEN
MADE, so that people are without excuse."

Yes, today I am so thankful for the wondrous gift of
nature and all it encompasses! What an amazing,
incredible love He has for us! He created all of this to
display His glory and majesty, sustain our earthly bodies,
and give us a place to live while we are here on earth.

Thankful Thursday #36

Today I am thankful for BEDS!

No, I am not thankful for them because I like to be lazy and lay around in them all day...quite the opposite.

I am thankful for beds because when the day is done and I have done all I could and worked hard, loved well, and served much, it is a place of respite and rejuvenation.

For me personally, having lived in my car before, only dreaming of a bed, it represents something even more. It represents a safe place to tuck away and know that I have a warm safe spot to be protected during the night. It is peace.

There are so many people in every country across the globe without a bed or even a cot to sleep on. Let's not take our beds for granted.

As an act of gratitude to God for giving me a bed, I love to joyfully make my bed every morning thanking Him for a beautiful place of rest…whether or not I slept well is beside the point you see.

It's about the gift of having a place to rest and appreciating it for just what it is…a gift!

If you aren't already in the practice of doing so, consider making your bed as soon as you get out of it as it enforces many things in your mind.

1. I am done lying down for the day…let's get this day started.
2. I am thankful to have a bed to sleep in; therefore, I will make it OUT OF GRATITUDE…an offering of worship and thankfulness to my God for giving it to me.
3. I want my bed to be a beautiful place of welcoming respite to sit and read a book during the day and when I get back into it at night.
4. I know that I have already done the first job of the day, which means I can do many more.
5. I can do small things with great love that emboldens me to go out in the world and do more things with great love.

So, you see it matters not whether it's a cot that you roll up, or a hammock that you tidy up, or a sleeping bag that you zip up and smooth out for the day. What matters is the heart of gratitude.

What we often forget in our daily routines is that there really is nothing routine about our routines. We see it as a routine, but it really is a beautifully orchestrated amount of time and space that has been given to us for only this one day.

Yes, the days add up to weeks and weeks to months and months to years, but we aren't promised a bed each of those days.

So, out of gratitude for having it right now, consider making your bed. We also forget sometimes that gratitude is a lot like love in that it's not a fuzzy feeling…it's an action. If I love someone, I will treat them so that they will know it. If I am thankful for something, I will act accordingly.

SCRIPTURES FOR THE DAY

LUKE 16:10 reminds us,
**"One who is FAITHFUL IN A VERY LITTLE IS ALSO
FAITHFUL IN MUCH, and one who is dishonest
in a very little is also dishonest in much."**

*Even though in biblical days they had roll up cots, and this verse is about
healing, notice it seems to be implied that making your bed (rolling
your mat in this case) should be a natural part of getting up.*

It's in ACTS 9:34,
**"Aeneas," Peter said to him, "Jesus Christ heals you.
GET UP AND ROLL UP YOUR MAT."
Immediately Aeneas got up.**

**Yes, I am thankful for beds! Look at your bed
or wherever you sleep in a whole new way
of gratitude and thank God for it!**

(And I am also thankful to wake up every morning thus far!)

Thankful Thursday #37

Today I am thankful for PAPER MACHE.

It is messy, sticky, takes time to make it well, and requires crazy amounts of glue and patience.

Have you ever made a paper mache bowl? I had not until recently and it literally brought me to worship-filled tears as I was making them. I was overcome with how very much it's like what our lives look like.

Here are the steps required.

1. Shred (with a long straight-cut shredder) tons of different colors and styles of paper.
2. Have a big work space that is covered with throw away tablecloths.
3. Have a big bowl of half white glue, half water mixture (mod podge).
4. Blow up a balloon to whatever size you wish your bowl to be and tie it off.
5. Poke a hole in a paper plate and turn the plate upside down and poke the tied end of the balloon through the hole to hold the balloon up as you work on it.
6. Now, one by one take each strip of paper and press it through the glue, then with your fingers squeeze all the excess glue off of it.
7. Then apply it to the top of the balloon (which will end up being the bottom of the bowl).

Here is why this craft brought me to literal tears and a worship filled moment of gratitude.

The bowls are so unique, so beautiful, and so completely awe inspiring once they are dried, the balloon is popped and peeled out, and any extra long strips are trimmed.

Like actually, they are stunning!

But the process…oh the process is so messy that sometimes you want to give up, just like life. You stay messy, you stay sticky, you don't know what you are doing half the time, and you are just hoping you are putting the right pieces in the right places for the idea of what you want it to look like.

I just became so overwhelmed thinking how our lives are so much like the process of making paper mache bowls.

They are messy. Sometimes, more often than not, it gets sticky, tough and not fun. There are so many different pieces we juggle and try to fit together the best we can, but are not sure we are doing it right.

In the process while it is drying (just like during our lives) it looks gross and the glue is dripping down the sides and the colors of the strips are all muted. Isn't that like life while we are here and in it? We sometimes feel as if everything we do leaves a trail of messes behind?

Here's the best part though my friend.
The next day (because it takes 24 hours to dry), when
I popped the balloons, peeled the balloons out, and set
them down to look at them, here is what I saw...

THEY LOOKED NOTHING LIKE THEY DID DURING
THE PROCESS!

THEY WERE STUNNING WORKS OF ART THAT WERE EACH SO
UNIQUE AND BEAUTIFULLY PUT TOGETHER AND NONE WERE
EXACTLY ALIKE...EVEN THE ONES THAT TRIED TO BE!

Just Like Each of US!

There is Hope my friend! Our lives look sticky and messy
and like we are messing it all up sometimes, but God is
doing something with our sticky messy stuff.
He is turning it into a beautiful piece of art!

SCRIPTURES FOR THE DAY

EPHESIANS 2:10 reminds us as we look at the paper mache bowl being crafted,
"For WE ARE HIS WORKMANSHIP, CREATED
IN CHRIST JESUS
for good works, which God prepared beforehand,
that we should walk in them."

ECCLESIASTES 3:11 reminds us of this,
"He has made EVERYTHING BEAUTIFUL IN ITS' TIME.
He has also set eternity in the human heart; yet
NO ONE CAN FATHOM WHAT GOD HAS DONE
from beginning to end."

**Yes, today I find myself so grateful for the process
of making paper mache bowls, and the beautiful
worship- filled perspective it provides.**

Thankful Thursday #38

Today I am thankful for PIPES!

Today I am thankful for something that most often goes unnoticed day in and day out and may even be seen by some as an annoying eyesore but without them we would be living an entirely different life.

Now you may be thinking…what in the world? She is reaching here.

Nope, not at all.

Remember this is about opening up the eyes of our soul and SEEING things that we too often take for granted.

So, if you were to pass by this old dirty pipe, you may think that it needs to be hosed off, or it should be covered up with something, or it needs to be replaced, or wonder if it is even in use anymore.

Let's take those perspective glasses out we like to refer to here and think about the completely different world that we would be living in without the crazy awesomeness of pipes!

Pipes carry water to and from our homes…whether to drink, water our plants, bathe in, and so much more. They also carry sewage AWAY from our homes…yes that's right…the stuff you may not want to talk about, but where would we be without that?! They also carry oil and other chemicals that we rely on for our daily transportation.

So, without those pipes, we wouldn't have water at the turn of the faucet in the sink, or bathroom. We wouldn't be able to flush our toilets. We wouldn't have access to gas our cars up for getting to where we need to go.

Yes, pipes are definitely under-appreciated.

How does this relate to life and scripture?

Oh, I am soooo glad you asked!

You see…what is it that pipes do? They carry what we need for everyday life to the places they need to go, right? Simply a supply line bringing us what we need.

So, why do we care what they look like, where they are, or if they are dirty or not?

So this is getting me giddy inside now!

Think about how many times in your life you can look back in hindsight and see clearly how God was using something you couldn't understand or appreciate at the time to get a message to you.

How often do we miss the message because we are so concerned about what the message carrier looks like?

We can be so caught up in "looking for how the message gets here" that we end up missing the message entirely.

Because all too often God uses ordinary, even easily missed means to get messages to us to see if we are REALLY LOOKING FOR HIM.

He uses His Word to give us messages, but we too often misinterpret or decide we only like certain parts of it.

He uses His very creation to witness to us the magnitude of His glory and yet we either tend to take that for granted, trash it, or worship the creation instead of The Creator.

He uses regular everyday people for massive greatness throughout all of history. But maybe we are busy waiting for a queen, king, or influencer that "looks like royalty" instead of seeing what He put right in front of us.

He gives us children, but often people get into heated discussions about the means of which they come into this world (regular, c section, or otherwise).

So often we can miss the supply itself because we were so
caught up in looking for a certain type of supply line.

It doesn't matter how He gets the message to us, but instead that He has pipelines of His messages set up all over the world and if we would just slow down and look we could see quite clearly the beauty of His pipelines that are all around us!

SCRIPTURE FOR THE DAY

Just as pipes supply some of our everyday needs,
PHILIPPIANS 4:19 tells us Christ provides for us all that we need.
"And my GOD WILL SUPPLY EVERY NEED OF YOURS
according to His riches in glory in Christ Jesus."
He doesn't say what the vessel will look like. Why does
that even matter? God uses what the world would call the
mundane throughout the entirety of history to reach people
of all nations and tribes to be brought to salvation.

Yes, today I am thankful for pipes as they represent that
God uses everyday, often unappreciated means to get His
message of love and forgiveness to all of the world.
They are so far from ordinary. It all
points to God...even the pipes!

Thankful Thursday #39

Today I am thankful for TRAVEL!

YES, Travel! It can look so different because it can be done locally, within the country, abroad, or even to the moon! It's such a massive word that encompasses an unfathomable amount of possibilities!

The only travel I really did growing up was to see our northern family members during the summer since my parents were both teachers and had the summers off. I LOVED traveling up there and getting away from my norm and seeing another part of the world.

Now that I am older and have my own family, we LOVE to travel and explore, even if it's local areas.

When we lived in the 2nd largest state in the country, we became big fans of traveling even just in our own state. There is such a big world out there and it's important and humbling to be able to spend time exploring it.

One of my favorite things about traveling, especially on a plane, is the humbling perspective it grants me.

It reminds me that I am a small piece of the picture and that God loves me still. It reminds me that there are billions and billions of other people that have families and struggles and to stay humble and kind.

It is good to be reminded that our life isn't the only or best way to do life. It is good to be humbled by other cultures and foods and ways of life. It is a reminder that God made all types of people in vastly different lands and we are not to be haughty with our own lives, somehow presuming it is better than another.

It is wonderful to be reminded that as beautiful as this world is and as amazing as the people are, the one thing that travel constantly reminds me is that *this is not our home.*

We are just sojourners traveling through this world. This is not our real home. Wherever we live, whether tent or mansion or anything in between… this is not our home.

That is a comforting reminder as well!

SCRIPTURES FOR THE DAY

LUKE 13:29 reminds us that God's people are everywhere!
**"People will come FROM EAST AND WEST
AND NORTH AND SOUTH,
and will take their places at the feast
in the Kingdom of God."**

PHILIPPIANS 3:20 reminds us of our true residency,
**"But OUR CITIZENSHIP IS IN HEAVEN,
and from it we await a Savior,
the Lord Jesus Christ,"**

AND

2 CORINTHIANS 5:1 continues to remind us of our real home,
**"For we know that if the tent that
is our earthly home is destroyed,
WE HAVE A BUILDING FROM GOD,
a house not made with hands,
ETERNAL IN THE HEAVENS."**

**Yes, I am thankful for travel. God made such a big
beautiful world, adorned it with special people that we
can learn from, and a creation that points us to Him.**

Thankful Thursday #40

Today I am thankful for
THOSE MOMENTS OF FEELING SMALL!

Today I am thankful for something that most people try to fight against.

Bare with me while I explain (don't worry, not in song and dance).

*Have you ever been truly afraid of something and just
wanted to cower under something and be kept safe?*

OR

Have you ever needed to feel there is something way bigger than
yourself so that you know there is something more?

I have felt the compelling longing to know that it's not all on me and that I can curl up and rest in knowing that I don't have to be "on" right now. I just want to be still and be.

Those are the moments feeling small can be
SO BIG AND COMFORTING!

I realize this all sounds counterproductive or counterintuitive so let's unpack it for a bit.

Just as in this picture with these massive trees towering over my family and they look so tiny and minuscule, so we sometimes maybe need to feel small in order to feel protected, seen and loved.

Think about it for a minute.

The world chases bigness right? They want the big social media accounts, the big crowds, the big lights, and the big fame...but then what? After all that has come and it is all big, then what do you have left to aim for?

I suggest to you that sometimes we need to feel small in order to feel special, loved, seen, protected, and known!

If I KNOW (and I do actually) that the God of the Universe...this massive incredible universe...SEES ME, then I actually feel quite comforted in all of that. I can be content and confident in feeling small and like I am His precious little child to look over and protect. Is it starting to make sense now?

If I am all big and have all this attention and glory and everyone can see me, it can be too much and overwhelming with no hope of comfort in sight.

It's the moments of feeling small that can actually make you feel the most seen, the most treasured, the most desired and loved ever! Think about it... relationships are like that right?

Our relationship with God is no different. Those one on one moments when you are having a soul connection with someone. It may seem small to the world and you may feel intimately connected, and those are the feeling small moments I am talking about!

When we were young and little, what did we want? To grow up and be big and in charge of our own lives, right? But, once we are grown, we realize it's not all it's cracked up to be. We sometimes wish for those feeling small moments of being a kid again, right? You can! That's how God sees us anyway!

Be confident enough to feel small and know that you are desired and loved by the massive King of the Universe who has got you!

SCRIPTURES FOR THE DAY

1 JOHN 2:1 reminds us we are little to Him and He has still got us,
"MY LITTLE CHILDREN,
I am writing these things to you so that you
may not sin. But if anyone does sin,
WE HAVE AN ADVOCATE WITH THE FATHER,
Jesus Christ The Righteous."

PSALM 32:7 reminds us we can run to him and be tucked away,
"You are a HIDING PLACE FOR ME;
YOU PRESERVE ME FROM TROUBLE;
You surround me with shouts of deliverance. Selah"

**Yes, I love those moments of feeling small and
protected when I need my Savior to cover me
from the rest of the world. Thank you God!**

Thankful Thursday #41

Today I am thankful for the
SURPRISE MOMENTS IN LIFE that turn out to be
something totally different than we imagine!

A while back we have had quite a few of these at our home, but I wanted to share one in particular with you.

When we lived in Texas, we were in an apartment and it was beautiful and we had no complaints. We had a couple of strange things happen, which I know from living many places can happen anywhere.

This most recent one was about 8 o'clock on a summer evening and the sun was just setting. The kids were in their room getting ready for bed.

Todd and I were in our bedroom folding laundry visiting and our conversation was broken up by a "tap, tap-tap-tap…tap" on our bedroom window.

This stopped us dead in our tracks because our bedroom window was also the window to our patio and a patio couch sat in front of our window. Anyway, we kind of looked at each other, took a breath and shrugged it off thinking it was some massive Texas size bug hitting the window.

It happened again and this time more distinct and clear and loud. We felt sure it was a person knocking this time. It didn't stop.

Instead of peeking directly out our blinds in case it was someone we didn't know, my husband decided to go around through the kitchen and peek through those blinds that also led to our patio.

A couple of seconds later he comes back in the room with a smile and says, "Babe, get your camera ready, but put it on silent and stand right here (he places me where he wants me to be). Be very still and don't make any sudden movements."

At this point I am excited but a little nervous at the no sudden movements part.

I follow all the instructions and am standing there holding my breath as he gently and quietly lifts up one of the top blinds on the bedroom window.

I see this beautiful little guy gently resting on our year round string lights that are hanging up on our patio window right above our couch.

He literally sat there and posed for me while I caught his picture and looked at me. We just stood there in awe at this little guy and this precious moment that God sent us to break us free from our usual routine to remind us what life is really all about.

He sat still on those light strands for probably a good solid minute letting us take in his beauty and the sweetness of the moment. Those are the special moments that I have to know are sent by God to remind us of the beauty in the journey.

As I was staring at this little guy and he allowed us to marvel at his beauty and simplicity, the verses below came to mind.

SCRIPTURES FOR THE DAY

MATTHEW 6:26-27 reminds us of this,
"LOOK AT THE BIRDS OF THE AIR;
they do not sow or reap or store away in barns,
and yet your Heavenly Father feeds them.
ARE YOU NOT MUCH MORE VALUABLE THAN THEY?
Can any one of you by worrying add a single hour to your life?"

JAMES 1:17 reminds us where all these surprise gifts come from,
"EVERY GOOD GIFT AND EVERY
PERFECT GIFT IS FROM ABOVE,
coming down from the Father of Lights with whom
there is no variation or shadow due to change."

Yes, I am so thankful for the sweet unexpected
moments that God gives us to remind us of the
beauty in the everyday moments that He longs
to surprise us with moment after moment.

Thankful Thursday #42

Today I am thankful for
PASSAGEWAYS OVER DANGEROUS TERRAIN!

So, the reason I am sharing this picture with you today is because while this may not look like treacherous terrain, it is some of the deadliest I assure you!

When we moved to Texas a few years back, I knew they had beaches, just like where we had previously lived in Alabama. But, what I didn't know is the danger that lies directly on their beaches!

In Texas, in their grassy area just before the sand, and even in the sand dunes themselves live one of the most well known and feared snakes…the rattlesnake.

WAIT…WHAT?!!! Yup…who knew right?

So, on many of the Texas beaches, they have these very long and elevated walkways built over the grassy rattlesnake areas and they even have signs (sometimes) warning to stay out…rattlesnake habitat!

I was shocked when we learned this the hard way. We had been picking up trash on a National Seashore one day as the girls wanted to earn their junior ranger badge. There was some trash like paper plates just at the edge of the dunes. The girls asked if they could go in there. Normally on dunes you see signs warning to stay out. It was just barely dune-ish, if you know what I mean. So, since I didn't see any signs and it was the edge of the dunes, I said, "Sure you can go grab that trash."

We must have spent a good half hour in that area.

When we came back to turn our trash in and get cleaned up, we told the ranger all about the trash in the first part of the edge of the dunes that we collected. She literally turned white.

I immediately assumed it was because we weren't supposed to be in the dunes. I told her we were very careful and didn't harm the dunes and didn't see any signs so we had assumed it was alright.

She replied with great shock, "No, you can't go near the dunes here because that's where the rattlesnakes live! And there are many of them!"

Then it was my turn to turn white and the kids looked at me and we all hugged and right away thanked God for protecting us.

So, even though there wasn't a "visible to the naked eye bridge" or passageway over the treacherous terrain that day, God did provide us safety that time through the dangerous area we didn't even know we were walking through.

He always provides a way out and will protect and guide you, although it may not look like it this side of heaven. There is an invisible army all around you that has got your back and He is providing a pathway for you!

SCRIPTURES FOR THE DAY

These 2 verses give me chills down to my soul thinking about how His love is so great that He should protect me like this.

PSALM 138:7 describes His presence all around us,
"THOUGH I WALK IN THE MIDST OF TROUBLE,
You will revive me;
You will stretch out Your hand
against the wrath of my enemies, and
YOUR RIGHT HAND WILL SAVE ME."

PSALM 91:7 is such an intimate portrait of His protection over us,
"A thousand may fall at your side, and
ten thousand at your right hand; but
IT SHALL NOT COME NEAR YOU."

Yes, I am so thankful for passageways over and through dangerous terrain that God provides all day, every day, whether or not we are even aware of them.

Thankful Thursday #43.

Today I am thankful for the SEAGULLS FLYING
SO HIGH IN THE SKY TOWARDS THE SUN!

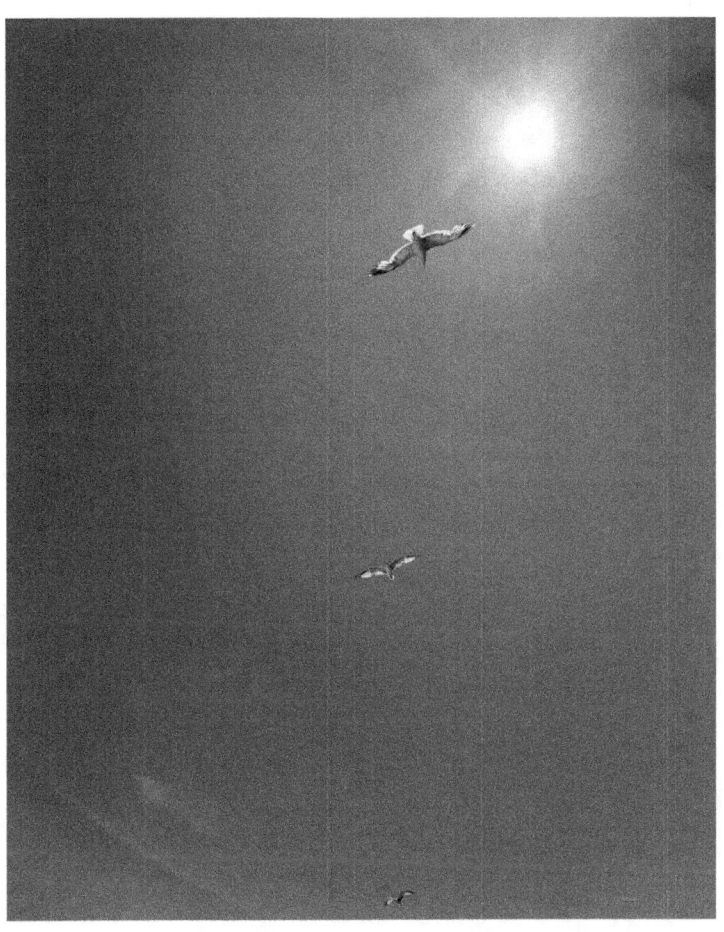

As our gaze is so often on what is in front of us, today, we are looking up for what we are grateful for!

Just as in this picture, it truly is a visual reminder of how we should be focused, especially on days that we may be tempted to get discouraged. We are to keep our gaze focused heavenwards towards the real Son!

I wonder how different my life would be if I would constantly 24/7, 365 keep my gaze that way!

I know it's hard…but the good stuff usually is, right?

I just love seeing how instincts kick in for the seagulls. If they feel danger or need to move…where do they go? They leave this world (or the ground anyway) and fly into the sky!

They soar and move around without weeping or complaining about it. It is simply part of who they are, how they are made, and what they are programmed to do.

We really are no different beloved. We are also programmed and made to fly heavenward…we just sometimes forget it in the regular business of everyday life!

Where do we go when we feel danger or threatened or scared? Do we look heavenward? Do we flee to Jesus and set our minds on Him? He gives us great comfort and promises peace if we choose that focus.

SCRIPTURES FOR THE DAY

PSALM 123:1 reminds us where our focus should be,
"TO YOU I LIFT UP MY EYES,
O You who are enthroned in the heavens!"

COLOSSIANS 3:2 instructs us,
"SET YOUR MINDS ON THINGS THAT ARE ABOVE,
not on things that are on earth."

JOHN 14:27 promises peace if we look to Him,
"Peace I leave with you; MY PEACE I GIVE TO YOU.
Not as the world gives do I give to you.
LET NOT YOUR HEARTS BE TROUBLED,
neither let them be afraid."

**Yes, I am thankful for the seagulls flying so high
towards the sun as a picture of how I should keep
my eyes focused heavenwards towards the Son!**

Thankful Thursday #44

Today I am thankful for CIRCLES and
the beautiful picture they paint!

Today I am thankful for a shape that encompasses everything, is every-where, and is constantly reminding us that it all comes together.

What a goofy thing to be thankful for you may be thinking. Not at all I would argue!

Let's take the shape of the earth, planets, sun and moon that God created Himself...all circles!

How about the shape of rings meant to fit perfectly on our fingers...circles!

Now let's go a little deeper and think of the meaning behind circles.

Circles are the perfect shape really because there is no beginning or middle or end. Not one side can claim to be bigger or more distinct or stand out among the rest of the shape. Nope...a circle is simply the perfect shape!

When we circle something on the calendar, or in our bible or in a book, what is our intention? We want to surround it and keep it separate from the rest, right? We are reminding ourselves it is extra special and want to come back to it and put our focus there.

Circles really are a picture of life and how it ebbs and flows...we can't disconnect one part of our life from the rest of it...it will all eventually connect and affect the other parts. It all eventually comes "full circle".

It all ends up connecting. It is all a part of this beautiful circle of life.

Everything inside a circle is enclosed, hemmed in, and surrounded much the same way that Jesus has a circle of love and protection all around us each and every moment of each and every day.

SCRIPTURES FOR THE DAY

PSALM 125:2 reminds us what God does for us with a circle!
"As the mountains surround Jerusalem, so
THE LORD SURROUNDS HIS PEOPLE
both now and forevermore."

PSALM 34:7 reminds us of the circle of protection,
"The angel of The Lord encamps AROUND
those who fear him, and delivers them."

JOB 26:10 even tells us about God forming His creation,
"He has inscribed a CIRCLE on the face of the waters
at the boundary between light and darkness."

Yes, today I am thankful for circles and how
they point to God when we look at them
through a Heavenly perspective.

Thankful Thursday #45

Today I am thankful for PEELING TREE BARK!

Did you know that when tree bark peels it's because the tree is growing and has
outgrown its skin? So it peels and sheds its bark to make way for new growth!

We depend on trees for so much; from shade and making paper, to making
furniture, and so much more! So, maybe it's time
to notice them and their growth!

Peeling tree bark is fascinating up close, as in this picture. The part peeling off may look old, wrinkly, hardened, and even dead. But do you see what's underneath? A beautiful, smooth, strong, even soft and very alive fresh skin!

This parallels our own life so much, right?

When we go through trials of different kinds and God is using that to grow us, sometimes, those dark, wrinkly, hardened ugly layers that were such a part of who we are, are being peeled away slowly. Sometimes we don't even notice it until they are gone and someone else comments on changes in our lives and attitudes. Or maybe we notice it all at once.

Peeling tree bark gives us hope that God does the same with us and is showing us that in His beautiful gift of creation and nature.

It can also teach us to be patient with others as their hardened layers maybe aren't ready to be shed just yet and love them anyway the way God loved us even when our shells were hard wrinkly, tough, and ugly.

SCRIPTURES FOR THE DAY

2 CORINTHIANS 3:18 describes the transformation!
"And WE ALL, who with unveiled faces contemplate the Lord's glory,
ARE BEING TRANSFORMED into His image
WITH EVER-INCREASING GLORY,
which comes from The Lord, who is the Spirit."

COLOSSIANS 3:10 reinforces what is happening
as your spiritual bark is peeling away,
"And have PUT ON THE NEW SELF,
WHICH IS BEING RENEWED in knowledge
after the image of Its Creator."

Yes, so very thankful for peeling tree bark as it paints
a picture of what is possible in our own lives and the
hope that God will peel away the hardened rough
spots and replace it with a beautiful newness!

Thankful Thursday #46

Today I am thankful for TRANSPARENCY.

I am thankful for what I can see through, whether for good or bad.

Do you ever walk by a painted over window or drive by a
car that has seriously dark tinted windows and you steer
clear because there is no way to know what's inside?

Transparency is a beautiful thing because for better or
for worse you can see clearly what is inside.

If we are made to encourage and lift one another up, transparency is a necessity. It can mean letting go of pain and baring old wounds, but that is what makes us relatable. Everyone has pain and hardships. It's when we are bold enough to bare it and be open and transparent with it that we can grow, become more emboldened in the faith, and come alongside others in their journey.

For those of you that are reading this who know me in real life know that I can be a bit chatty and up front, if we click that is. It's because I have stayed too trapped in my own head listening to the lies of the world for too long and I want out. I am tearing down the tinting so you can clearly see what you are getting, for better or for worse.

It's totally OK if you don't like it because you can tell me and I can move on.

If you are ever window shopping and just strolling by different shops, what do you do? Well, maybe you stop, peek through the window, see what the merchandise is, and if interested you may enter the store or plan to come back another time. If you aren't interested, you still appreciate the transparency of knowing ahead of time what was in there. And, then you simply move on. No feelings get hurt. It's just personal preference.

I believe we were made for transparency. I also know that we won't all have the same style or personality. I am too chatty for some. I am too personal for some. I still like those people and totally respect them if they choose to move on from me.

I won't change being transparent just because they don't like what is inside. Just the same way a store won't change that it carries instruments if you were looking for clothing, right?

Be thankful for transparency and the gift it gives you of allowing you to know what you are walking into.

Consider Jesus, His entire life here on earth, the Psalms and the Bible in its entirety.

All of it SCREAMS TRANSPARENCY! If the Bible wasn't transparent telling us what to do, how we are to behave, who Jesus is and who we are in Him, how in the world would we have any hope?

Transparency gives us HOPE!

SCRIPTURES FOR THE DAY

EPHESIANS 4:25 encourages us to tear the tinting off of our lives,
"Therefore, having PUT AWAY FALSEHOOD,
let each one of you
SPEAK THE TRUTH WITH HIS NEIGHBOR,
for we are members one of another."

JOHN 8:32 reminds us what being transparent can do,
"And you will know the truth, and
THE TRUTH WILL SET YOU FREE."

Today, let's be grateful for the beauty of
transparency and what it allows us to see,
whether we like it or not. Transparency is a
courageous step towards freedom in Christ!

Thankful Thursday #47

Today I am thankful for TIME.

Today I am thankful for something so fleeting. It is something never tangible except in pictures. Something that we never know how much we will get of it. It's the most priceless commodity in the world!

Aahh...yes, the fleeting, never slowing down, no matter who you
are or where you come from unapologetic nature of time.

Time is the one thing that no matter how we spend it, we can never get it back or get more of it. The more we spend it, the less we have of it.

It moves on whether we are awake or asleep.

It makes up the moments in our life.

I am thankful for it because it is by time that we measure the seconds, moments, days, and years of our lives.

Through time we are thankful for celebrations like birthdays and holidays.

Time is the most precious commodity we could imagine as each second is a life filled gift that can be used for good, bad, indifferent, or anything in between.

One thing it can never be is stagnant.

The ticking of the clock is a constant reminder to not be idle or wasteful with our time, and yet to be thankful that the time here is definitely limited as well.

SCRIPTURES FOR THE DAY

COLOSSIANS 4:5 reminds us to be wise with this beautiful gift,
"**Walk in wisdom toward outsiders,**
MAKING THE BEST USE OF THE TIME."

ECCLESIASTES 3:1 reminds us time is appointed,
"**For everything there is a season,**
AND A TIME FOR EVERY MATTER UNDER HEAVEN:"

Yes, I am thankful for the precious commodity of time! Each second is another opportunity to show love, serve well, and live joyfully.

Thankful Thursday #48

Today I am thankful for MODERN MEDICAL EQUIPMENT!

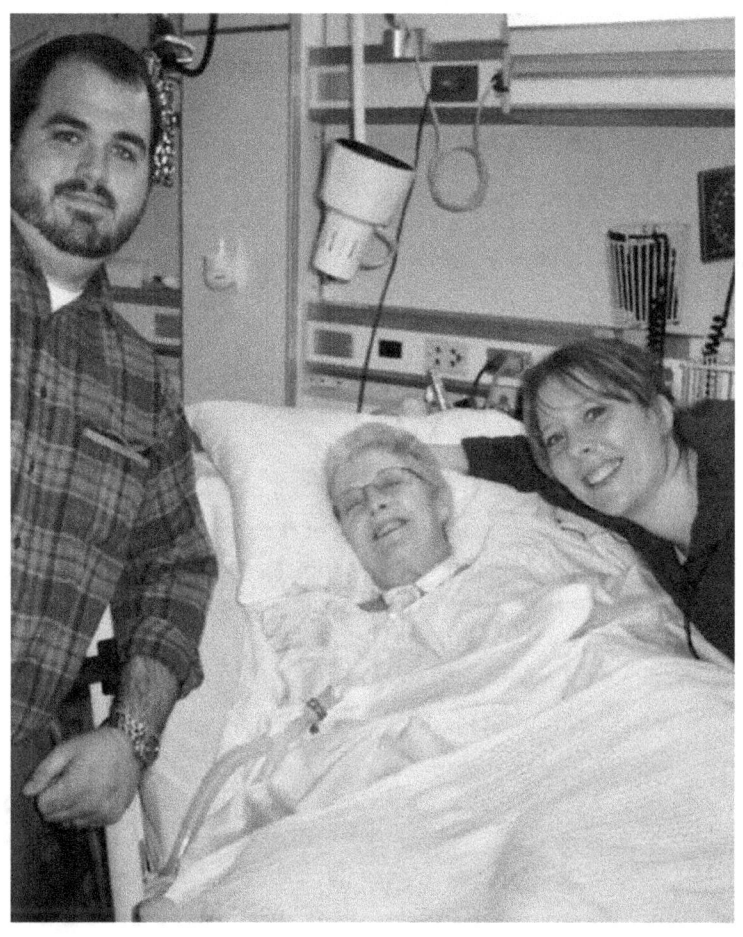

Today I am thankful for something that hasn't always been around and isn't available everywhere, but when it is, it can be a real blessing.

This may sound a bit silly to those of you that know me as I love to be as natural and back to basics as I can with my homemade DIY cough syrups and Essential Oil cleaners and Oil Cleansing Face Washing.

But here is the deal.

There is a time and a place for all types of medicine, whether homeopathic, eastern or western and it all depends on what the body and the patient needs. Different levels of care demand certain interventions.

There are so many places in the world where these needed types of equipment still aren't available so I want to be thankful for them while we have them.

I have personally used so much of this equipment during my time as an EMT and watch it sustain lives or even bring people back to life.

My mom wouldn't have survived the life flight ride to the hospital without modern medical equipment, nor any of the surgeries or the rest of her nearly 10 years of life, living as a C1 quadriplegic, without a countless array of medical equipment that would become her new basic necessities. She required a ventilator and a countless list of equipment just for daily life.

My 2nd child and I wouldn't be here without modern medical intervention.

For the past few years I have required emergency breathing treatments or I wouldn't be here either.

How many times do we take for granted the amazing minds that God grants wisdom to to come up with crazy inventions that should allow us to live longer and expand our horizons to the possibilities of growth and life?

SCRIPTURE FOR THE DAY

PROVERBS 18:15 reminds us,
"The HEART OF THE DISCERNING ACQUIRES KNOWLEDGE,
for the ears of the wise seek it out."

**Let's be thankful for the gift of modern medical
equipment and that God should allow
such wisdom to enter our minds!**

Thankful Thursday #49

Today I am thankful for
THE MUSIC THAT IS EVERYWHERE!

*I love music and am thankful for all kinds from classical and country to rock
and hip-hop and everything in between, but there's something more!*

There is music in nature and all around us too…we just have to have ears to hear.

*The crickets chirping in unison in the evening together
filling the air with a soft, clicking rhythm.*

The birds chirping and making beautiful melodies.

The rhythm of our feet hitting the stair stepper in unison in the gym.

Music is everywhere my friend! Just open your heart and mind and the ears of your soul to hear it all!

I could literally hear music anywhere, even in the quiet...the gentle beat of the air conditioning blowing, or the leaves rustling outside. I often tap my hands to my thighs or rock back and forth to the beat in the grocery store or other places you may not expect to find people "hearing music".

Music is such a blessing because it's the invisible but audible language that crosses all barriers of cultures and dialects to reach down deep into the depths of our soul where we all understand its meaning.

Music is the song of our souls...and it connects us all!

Open your ears and hear music where you are right now...is it the clicking of the keyboard, the elevator music while you are on hold, the tapping of the pencil, the music in the gym?

Music is everywhere and what a blessing it is...it gives our days rhythm and a mutual connection that we all immediately understand!

SCRIPTURES FOR THE DAY

EPHESIANS 5:19 instructs us to make music,
"speaking to one another with psalms,
hymns, and songs from the Spirit.
Sing and MAKE MUSIC FROM YOUR HEART
to The Lord,"

PSALM 95:1b is a reminder that music is to be joyful,
"let us MAKE A JOYFUL NOISE
to The Rock of our salvation!"

Yes, today I am thankful for music and the many forms
it comes in throughout everyday moments. Where will
you hear music today and be thankful when you hear it?

Thankful Thursday #50

Today I am thankful for MORNINGS,
because they are new beginnings!

Today I am thankful for something that some people dread and even complain about. I'm not sure why though because they are an incredible gift!

We all love a good triumph story of overcoming, right?

How do most of those stories go?

There are enough hardships and trials and then morning comes…the new beginning and things are somehow different and this time they get it right!

Mornings are a beautiful testament to God's grace to us, in that we are allowed to wake up and start anew all over again!

It's the opportunity to rise up, thank Him for the gift of another day, and tackle it hard and all in with great fervor!

We all love a new beginning like New Years or birthdays and that's exactly what mornings are every single day!

We just need to take our perspective glasses out and look at mornings in a whole new light!

SCRIPTURES FOR THE DAY

PSALM 143:8 tells us where our focus should be in the morning,
"LET ME HEAR IN THE MORNING OF YOUR STEADFAST
LOVE, for in you I trust. MAKE ME KNOW THE WAY
I SHOULD GO, for to you I lift up my soul."

LAMENTATIONS 3:22-23 reminds us of the mornings promise,
"The steadfast love of The Lord never ceases;
HIS MERCIES never come to an end;
THEY ARE NEW EVERY MORNING;
great is your faithfulness."

*PSALM 30:5b reminds us that even when times are
rough, mornings offer a fresh vantage point,*
"Weeping may tarry for the night, but
JOY COMES WITH THE MORNING."

**Today let's take out our perspective glasses and look at
mornings in a whole new light and be grateful for the
mercy-dripping opportunity they are to start fresh!**

Thankful Thursday #51

Today I am crazy thankful for CHANGE!

Today I am so very grateful for something I used to hate and dread. I didn't want to go through it no matter that I knew it was inevitable.

Change used to be super hard for me because it was my comfort zone.
It was the only thing I knew and no matter if it was bad or good,
I just didn't want things to be different.
I was comfortable clinging to what I knew and didn't want to let go.

What I have learned is that change IS GOING TO HAPPEN regardless of whether or not I like it or want it to.

The best part of what I have learned is there are usually truly amazing rewards and blessings just waiting on the other side of that change! Trust The One who is leading the way through the changes. Trust the process and know that it really will all work out in the end!

After all, He is the one who designed the seasons and they, at their very core, are change! There will always be a changing of the seasons. He designed us to be born, grow up, hopefully grow old, and eventually die. Change will come regardless if I welcome it or not.

It can mean a walking away from something you thought was your forever.

It can mean walking towards something you know nothing about, but are called to it regardless.

Change has unlimited faces, which is actually exciting!

I used to dig my heels in when my husband and I first got married and moved a few times…the first 5 years I think we moved 7 times…then slowed down a bit and have only moved a total of 11 times in 19 years (now embarking on our 12th in 23 years).

The old me would have been like, "OK we are good now. We have a good life and need to stay put."

BUT GOD.

Oh the change He can work in our hearts as well as our lives.

Now, knowing what I know...that we have been blessed with truly amazing soul connection friends in so many places whom we love with our whole hearts. Knowing that life has been good wherever we have lived, and that God provided for us regardless...makes me excited for possible moves in the future.

I know that I won't live forever and that the world is bigger than my understanding and there are truly amazing people all over the place. There are people in my life now I can't imagine moving away from, but it has been that way wherever we have lived really.

My husband's favorite saying is
"life begins outside of your comfort zone."
If that is the case, then I must be fully living because I have
been ripped away from it more times than not.

I can now say I fully agree with that statement as it is where growth, faith
in action, and overcoming takes place...outside of the comfort zone.

Change is going to happen whether you are ready for it or not.
Change is coming. Here is the best part...there is something really
wonderful waiting to greet you on the other side of that change!

It really will all be OK post change...don't be afraid and dread it...open your heart and mind and welcome it as you step out of your comfort zone into a world of possibilities.

SCRIPTURES FOR THE DAY

ISAIAH 43:19 tells us,
"See, I AM DOING A NEW THING!
Now it springs up; do you not perceive it?
I AM MAKING A WAY IN THE WILDERNESS
and streams in the wasteland."

What we see as change, God views as His plan.
JEREMIAH 29:11 reminds us what those plans are,
"For I know THE PLANS I HAVE FOR YOU,"
declares The LORD,
"plans to prosper you and not to harm you,
PLANS TO GIVE YOU HOPE AND A FUTURE."

**Yes, today I am very thankful for change and
the opportunities, hope, and growth that
lie waiting on the other side of it.**

Thankful Thursday #52

Today I am thankful for the beautiful gift of
LIFE AND BEING ALIVE!

Welcome to the last Thankful Thursday for the year!

What else could be more fitting to wrap this book up with than the thankfulness for the GIFT OF LIFE!

May we never take for granted that we are even here;
whether injured, able-bodied, special needs, rich, poor,
sick, or healthy...SIMPLY BEING ALIVE!

Just the fact that you and I are even here. We could have been anything else. We could have been a dog or a paper clip, but no...we get to actually exist as humans and have this temporary, amazing, once-in-a-lifetime, irreplaceable gift of LIFE!

All the incredible things that have to come together just for us to be able to be born and then live and breathe the 30,000 times a day that we breathe every day of our lives.

So many things we take for granted like the act of breathing...oh, life...how in the world do we show gratitude for something so mind boggling as this?

We first realize its gravity and magnitude by thinking of it like this.

What if someone asked you what do you want? You can have ANYTHING AT ALL that you want no matter the price or the size or the unbelievable nature of it all.

DREAM BIG!

Would you wish for tons of land with lots of animals? Would you wish for getting all the homeless people off the street? Would you wish for your own private island where you can visit anytime you want on your own private jet? Would you wish to have the money to travel to any country any time you wish?

BOOM...IT'S YOURS!

OK...so maybe not really, but think of life like that except there is one catch...

You can have this incredible gift, but there's no guarantee how long it will last...maybe it's a day..maybe it's a month...maybe it's 100 years.

Well, that is a little bit like God's gift of life to us. We are given this ONE LIFE. We aren't told how long it will last. One thing we do know is that it won't last forever. We are told we can do anything we want with it.

But because you don't know when it will go away, you have to be sure not to become like a child the day after Christmas...disenchanted with their new toy and no longer fascinated by it.

Life is the most mind blowing incredible gift anyone could ever hope for! It's not about whether it's good or bad...just literally BEING ALIVE!

I am so thankful you were born, and are alive and present right now. Please know that you were designed for a reason and a purpose and God doesn't make mistakes (*it's actually the one thing He can't do!*).

Let the gratitude of Life and Being Alive hit you in the heart, soul, and mind and reverberate throughout your entire being deep into your soul's fibers!

SCRIPTURES FOR THE DAY

GENESIS 2:7 describes the awe inspiring way He created the first human being,
"Then THE LORD GOD FORMED THE MAN
of dust from the ground and
BREATHED INTO HIS NOSTRILS THE BREATH OF LIFE,
and the man became a living creature."

1 CORINTHIANS 15:39 reminds us yet again how unique being a human being is,
"FOR NOT ALL FLESH IS THE SAME, but there is one kind for
humans, another for animals, another for birds, and another for fish."

HEBREWS 12:28 reminds us why we should seek to
have a posture of gratitude, **"Therefore, since we are**
receiving a kingdom that cannot be shaken,
LET US BE THANKFUL AND SO
WORSHIP GOD ACCEPTABLY
with reverence and awe,"

May your day and life be filled with awestruck gratitude
for the unbelievable gift of your one of a kind life
and thanksgiving for the rest of your journey!

Scripture Reference

#1 Shadows
Psalm 63:7
Psalm 36:7
Isaiah 9:2

#2 My Person
James 4:8a
I John 3:1a
Hebrews 4:15

#3 Messy Moments
Colossians 3:14
Ecclesiastes 3:12

#4 Seashells
Psalm 34:18
2 Corinthians 12:9

#5 Tree Trunks
Psalm 96:12
Psalm 32:8

#6 Fade and Blur Effect
Psalm 36:1
Isaiah 43:25
Romans 8:1

#7 Air
Job 33:4
John 3:8
2 Corinthians 5:5

#8 Sleep
Psalm 127:2
Psalm 4:8
Psalm 121:4

#9 Piggyback Rides
Deuteronomy 31:8
Psalm 139:5
Joshua 1:9
Psalm 68:19

#10 Freedom
Galatians 5:1
Galatians 5:13
2 Corinthians 3:17
Romans 8:2

#11 Imagination
Genesis 2:19-20
Revelation 9
Matthew 18:3

#12 Perspective
Psalm 139
2 Corinthians 4:18
1 Samuel 16:7b

#13 Contrast of Light and Darkness
Psalm 18:28
John 1:5
John 8:12
John 12:46

#14 Setbacks In Life
Isaiah 40:29
Isaiah 41:10
2 Timothy 1:7

#15 Changing Of The Clouds
2 Corinthians 5:17
Ezekiel 36:26
Romans 12:2
Hebrews 13:8

#16 Stairs
2 Peter 3:9
Philippians 1:6

#17 Pets
Jeremiah 8:7
Proverbs 6:6-8
Proverbs 12:10

#18 Rain
Joel 2:23
Job 5:10

#19 Snow
Psalm 51:7
Matthew 28:3

#20 The Cross
Hebrews 12:28
Colossians 2:14

#21 Our Differences
Galatians 3:28
1 Peter 3:8
John 13:34-35

#22 The Valleys
Psalm 23:4
Romans 5:3-5

#23 Rooftops
Psalm 59:1
Psalm 91:4

#24 Doorways
Matthew 7:7
Revelation 3:8

#25 Footprints
Genesis 28:15
Philippians 3:12-14
2 Corinthians 5:7

#26 Sea Turtles
I Corinthians 15:51-57

#27 Today
James 4:13-14
Matthew 6:11
Psalm 118:24

#28 Tattoos
Isaiah 49:16
1 Peter 1:18-19

#29 Dilapidated Old Buildings
Psalm 147:3
1 Peter 5:10
2 Corinthians 4:16-17

#30 One Way Signs
Ephesians 2:8-9
John 14:6

#31 Dancing
Psalm 149:3
2 Samuel 6:14a
Psalm 30:11a

#32 Exercise
Romans 12:1
1 Corinthians 6:9-10

#33 Microscopes
Psalm 139:15
1 Corinthians 2:9-10

#34 Trashcans
2 Corinthians 10:4-5
Psalm 103:12

#35 Nature
1 Timothy 4:4
Romans 1:20

#36 Beds
Luke 16:10
Acts 9:34

#37 Paper Mache
Ephesians 2:10
Ecclesiastes 3:11

#38 Pipes
Philippians 4:19

#39 Travel
Luke 13:29
Philippians 3:20
2 Corinthians 5:1

#40 Feeling Small
1 John 2:1
Psalm 32:7

#41 Surprise Moments In Life
Matthew 6:26-27
James 1:17

#42 Passageways Over Dangerous Terrain
Psalm 138:7
Psalm 91:7

#43 Seagulls Flying Towards The Sun
Psalm 123:1
Colossians 3:2
John 14:27

#44 Circles
Psalm 125:2
Psalm 34:7
Job 26:10

#45 Peeling Tree Bark
2 Corinthians 3:18
Colossians 3:10

#46 Transparency
Ephesians 4:25
John 8:32

#47 Time
Colossians 4:5
Ecclesiastes 3:1

#48 Modern Medical Equipment
Proverbs 18:15

#49 Music That Is Everywhere
Ephesians 5:19
Psalm 95:1b

#50 Mornings
Psalm 143:8
Lamentations 3:22-23
Psalm 30:5b

#51 Change
Isaiah 43:19
Jeremiah 29:11

#52 The Gift Of Life and Being Alive
Genesis 2:7
1 Corinthians 15:39
Hebrews 12:28

About the Author

Susan Brown wrote *One Year Of Thankful Thursdays* from a place of deep desperation for Jesus and an unquenchable desire for more than this world could offer her. From homeless, depressed, and overwhelmed to a joy-filled, successful, multi-faceted entrepreneur who longs to serve others, Susan is a mother to 2 amazing girls, and wife to her best friend for over 22 years. Her love for others and her calling, led her and her husband to co-found Legacy Game Changers, LLC. Their mission is to equip visionary believers to create and live out a game changing legacy that transforms generations to come! She has a special heart for those that against all odds and rationale continue to choose hope and move forward. She and her husband also renovate houses and are actively involved in supporting the homeless in their community. She loves to travel and speak to radically encourage others towards overcoming and transforming their beautiful one-of-a-kind life, and become a Legacy Game Changer.

A note from the author:
I would love to hear from you and you are always welcome to email me at hello@legacygamechangers.com

Main Websites:
LegacyGameChangers.com
Susan-Brown.com

Hire Susan To Speak:
SusanBrownSpeaks.com

Free Gift For You

Susan shares some of her trade secrets here as a FREE GIFT for you! Introducing the Ultimate Guide to Cultivating a Heart of Gratitude and Discovering God in Every Moment!

Want to know HOW TO get to a place of Gratitude in a practical way?

Susan unveils 5 of her daily secret tips here to share with you on your journey!

Curated by Susan Brown

5 Steps To Cultivating a Heart of Gratitude

FREE GIFT FOR YOU!

Go to *BonusGiftFromSusan.com* to grab yours now!

Susan BROWN

More From Susan

The Peace Of Mind System

PEACEOFMINDBLUEPRINT.COM

#1

FOUNDATIONAL GO-TO RESOURCE TO PROTECT YOUR FAMILY, LIFE'S WORK, AND RADICALLY TRANSFORM YOUR FUTURE

"I feel like this weight of "what if" stress has been lifted. This is truly a gift to the world and I am so thankful I stumbled upon it."

-Rose Parma
Christian Life/Biz Mentor

"What more could you ask for? The most important Guidebook You'll Ever Need"

-Wendy Wallace
Christian Life Coach